Discovering Fiction

A Reader *of* North American Short Stories

AN INTRODUCTION

- Judith Kay

- Rosemary Gelshenen

CAMBRIDGE
UNIVERSITY PRESS

CAMBRIDGE UNIVERSITY PRESS
Cambridge, New York, Melbourne, Madrid, Cape Town, Singapore,
São Paulo, Delhi, Dubai. Tokyo, Mexico City

Cambridge University Press
32 Avenue of the Americas, New York, NY 10013–2473, USA
www.cambridge.org
Information on this title: www.cambridge.org/9780521703901

First published 2008
4th printing 2011

Printed in Hong Kong, China, by Golden Cup Printing Company Limited

A catalog record for this publication is available from the British Library.

Library of Congress Cataloging in Publication Data

Discovering fiction : a reader of North American short stories : an introduction / [edited by] Judith Kay
[and] Rosemary Gelshenen.
    p. cm. -- (Discovering fiction.)
  Includes index.
  ISBN 978-0-521-70390-1
1. English language--Textbooks for foreign speakers. 2. United States--Social life and
customs--Ficiton. 3. Canada--Social life and customs--Ficiton. 4. Short stories, American. 5. Short
stories, Canadian. I. Kay, Judith. II. Gelshenen, Rosemary.
PE1128.D484 2008
428.6'4--dc22

                          2007051329

ISBN-13 978-0-521-70390-1 pack consisting of student's book and audio CD
ISBN-13 978-0-521-70391-8 teacher's manual

Art direction and book design: Adventure House, NYC
Layout services: Page Designs International
Audio production: Full House, NYC
Cover illustration: Chris O'Leary
Illustrations: Dan Brown: The Luck of Roaring Camp, The Californian's Tale, The Tree of
Knowledge; Alicia Hough: A Pair of Silk Stockings, The Pace of Youth; Rob Lawson: Young Man
Axelbrod, Its Wavering Image; Tim Otis: One Thousand Dollars, The Mask of the Red Death, All
the Years of Her Life; Ruth Palmer: David Swan, The Legend of Sleepy Hollow.

About the Authors

JUDITH KAY has extensive experience teaching writing, communication skills, and grammar. She taught at Marymount Manhattan College in New York City, where she and Rosemary Gelshenen were colleagues. She now lives in Florida, where she has taught at Lynn University and Broward Community College. In addition, Kay has given seminars in writing, and Kay and Gelshenen have presented workshops at regional and international meetings of TESOL (Teaching English to Speakers of Other Languages).

Kay has a master's degree in TESOL from Hunter College in New York City and is a member of Phi Beta Kappa. She is also a writer of short stories and novellas.

ROSEMARY GELSHENEN teaches literature, creative writing, and grammar in New York City at both Marymount Manhattan College and New York University. Formerly, she taught English at Norman Thomas High School and was a teacher trainer for the New York City Board of Education. Her awards include the Veritas Medal for Excellence in Education (1986) and New York City Teacher of the Year (1983). She also received two Impact II grants for innovative methods in teaching.

Gelshenen's articles on teaching methods have appeared in numerous educational publications, and she lectures on literary topics. She is the author of *Instant English Literature* (1994), a lighthearted approach to the lives and works of nineteenth century English novelists.

Contents

PART THREE   MYSTERY AND FANTASY   86

Chapter 7 ▪ *The Californian's Tale* MARK TWAIN _____ 88

To the Instructor

Discovering Fiction, An Introduction, features 12 universally appealing and engaging short stories that have been specially adapted to be accessible to students who are at the pre-intermediate level. Accompanying these stories are lessons that include vocabulary, comprehension, grammar, summarizing, and writing activities. In addition, there are tasks that teach students how to understand and analyze the stories and thus develop an appreciation for literature.

Discovering Fiction, An Introduction, is organized into four thematic parts – *Making Choices, The Role of Fate, Mystery and Fantasy*, and *Close Relationships*. There are three chapters in each part. Each chapter has one short story that revolves around the part's theme. The stories are adaptations of original stories written by American and Canadian authors in the late 1800s and early 1900s. Each chapter presents vocabulary, grammar, and a literary term that all come from or are related to the story.

Several options are possible for working through the book, depending upon the needs of your students or the amount of time you have for your classes. You could work through the Student's Book from beginning to end, or you could pick and choose parts and chapters. While the stories can be read out of sequence, note that the grammar is presented in a sequential fashion, beginning with basic parts of speech, such as nouns, adjectives, and adverbs in Part One; followed by count and noncount forms, articles, and pronouns in Part Two, and verb forms in Part Three; and ending with sentence structure in Part Four. The literary terms are also presented sequentially from simple concepts to more complicated ones.

The following provides information on the four main sections of each chapter – *Pre-Reading, The Story, After Reading*, and *Thinking about the Story* – and the review section – *Summing Up* – at the end of each part. It also lists items in the *Appendix*, with information about the audio CD at the back of the Student's Book. (Detailed suggestions for teaching all of the activities in the Student's Book are available in the Teacher's Manual, which may be purchased separately.)

PRE-READING

To generate interest before reading a story, students are asked to use their own knowledge and experience to answer questions related to the general topic of the story. Then, using their imaginations, students discuss the illustration on the first page of the chapter, which depicts a specific scene from the story.

In preparation for reading the story, students learn key vocabulary, idioms, and expressions that are in the story. They read a brief preview of the story plot and make predictions about what will happen. Note that the Story Preview is recorded on the audio CD that can be found at the back of each book. If you wish, you can play the Story Preview and then ask students to predict what will happen.

At the end of the Pre-Reading section, students are introduced to a literary term. Students are then asked to think about how this literary term can be applied to the story as they read.

The Story

Before reading a story, students read a brief biography of the author. If possible, try to provide students with further information to help them understand the historical period in which the story was written. Students then read the story. They should be encouraged to read the story the first time without looking up words in the dictionary. Students should guess the meanings of the words from the context. They can circle or underline unfamiliar words to look up after they have read the story. The lines in each story are numbered for easy reference.

After Reading

After reading the story, students first check and discuss their understanding of the story by answering several comprehension questions. Students then work on a vocabulary comprehension activity, which helps students develop their vocabulary acquisition skills. Students can find the target vocabulary words in the story and are encouraged to guess the meanings in context.

This section ends with a grammar activity. A boxed explanation gives basic information on one grammar structure, with examples from the story. Two practice exercises help students apply what they have learned from the grammar explanation.

Thinking About the Story

In this last section of each chapter, students are asked to think about the story on a deeper level. By answering and discussing inferential questions, students share what the story means to them. Students also complete a task that has them "read between the lines," which helps them better understand the true meaning of the author's words.

Students then use the literary term they learned in the Pre-Reading section to analyze the story. Each chapter uses a different graphic organizer to guide students through their analyses of the story and help them build on observations they have made while reading.

Finally, to conclude the chapter, students arrange a list of sentences into a summary of the story and share their overall thoughts about the story in a writing task.

SUMMING UP

At the end of each part, the Summing Up section reviews the theme, vocabulary, and grammar of the three chapters in that part. This section helps students see thematic links among the stories.

The Summing Up section ends with an *Elements of a Short Story* chart. This chart has students analyze the stories in terms of the five basic elements of a short story: setting, character, plot, conflict, and theme. The chart in the Summing Up section has been partially filled out for one of the stories. You can ask students to complete this chart for that story and/or you can photocopy the blank chart on page xvii and have students fill it out for one or both of the other stories in the part they have just finished.

APPENDIX

The Appendix includes a complete list of literary terms and a complete list of all the words, idioms, and expressions that are in the book. It also includes an index to help locate the stories, authors, literary terms, and grammar presented in each chapter.

STUDENT'S BOOK AUDIO CD

An audio CD is packaged into the back of this book. It contains readings from all 12 of the stories. In addition, the Story Preview from each chapter is included. The reading from the story picks up where the Story Preview leaves off, so that students can listen to the Story Preview, predict what will happen, and then listen to see if their prediction proved accurate. One way you can use this CD is to do the prereading in class, and have students predict the ending. Then you can have them listen to the story at home before reading it.

To the Student

The 12 short stories in *Discovering Fiction, An Introduction*, are a fun way to learn about literature or fiction and improve your English. By using this book, you will:

- increase your vocabulary
- review and practice grammar
- discuss the stories with other students
- relate the stories to your own experiences
- learn the basic elements and literary terms of short stories

We hope you enjoy discovering the world of fiction while you improve your English.

Acknowledgments

We wish to thank the following people for their interest in and dedication to bringing forth this new edition to the *Discovering Fiction* series – *Discovering Fiction, An Introduction*.

For their thoughtful and useful feedback, we thank the following reviewers: Joanne K. Beard, Proctor High School, Utica, New York; Bernadette Mizicko Beler, Kent State University; Linda Felzer, Pacifica High School, Oxnard, California; Paula Flores, Instituto Tecnológico y de Estudios Superiores de Monterrey (ITESM); and Dr. Thomas Meyer, Miami Dade Community College.

For the editing and production of this book, we thank Bernard Seal, Commissioning Editor, for supporting our original ideas and encouraging us through the process. We thank Karen McAlister Shimoda, Development Editor, for her devotion to the project and for her patience. We thank Sylvia Dare, Senior Project Editor, for checking the fine details and keeping all of us on schedule.

We also thank Angela Castro, Development Editor, for her work on Part Three; Ann Pascoe-Van Zyl, Development Editor, for her feedback on the literary term exercises; and Leslie De Jesus and Carlos Rountree for their all-around administrative support.

Finally, we owe a special thanks to the teachers who first taught us how to read.

You opened our eyes and minds.
You gave us the wonder of stories.

JUDITH KAY AND ROSEMARY GELSHENEN

Elements of a Short Story Chart

Name _____ Date _____

Choose a story to analyze and write its name on the blank line in the chart. Then complete the chart with a few sentences for each of the elements: *setting*, *characters*, *plot*, *conflict*, and *theme(s)*.

Elements of _____

(name of story)

SETTING

CHARACTERS

PLOT

CONFLICT

THEME(S)

PART ONE

Making Choices

Chapter 1

YOUNG MAN AXELBROD
– Sinclair Lewis

Chapter 2

A PAIR OF SILK STOCKINGS
– Kate Chopin

EVERY DAY, we all make choices about what to do with our day or with our lives. Some choices we make are small, such as what to eat, what to wear, or what to do that day. Other choices we make are big and can lead to our success or failure, our happiness or disappointment. Characters in literature, as in real life, also have to make choices.

In the three stories you are about to read, an elderly man chooses what to do after he retires, a housewife chooses how she will spend some money she saved, and a young man chooses what to do with $1,000 from his uncle. As you read these stories, ask yourself if you agree with the choices the characters make. What choices would you make if you were the three characters?

Chapter 3

ONE THOUSAND DOLLARS

– O. Henry

Chapter 1
Young Man Axelbrod SINCLAIR LEWIS

A | PRE-READING

1. Think Before You Read

Answer the following questions.

1. Why do people go to college?
2. What should someone do to prepare for college?
3. What are the qualities of a good college student?
4. How do you feel when you have a much older student in one of your classes?

2. Picture Focus

With a partner, talk about the picture.

Who are the two men? Where are they going?

3. Key Vocabulary

Study the following key words from the story. They all relate to *going to college*. Then complete the paragraph using each word once.

> **scholar** a person who studies and loves learning; a person who has a lot of knowledge
>
> **knowledge** information that someone receives from experience or studying
>
> **degree** a title given by a college or university for completing a program of courses
>
> **grades** scores from a test or a course, using the letters A, B, C, D, or F
>
> **literature** books, stories, poems, plays, etc., with artistic value
>
> **assignments** work or study that you must do for a class

There are many students who go to a college or university just to get a

_____. But a true _____ is someone who studies

because he or she has a love of learning. Perhaps such students study

_____ so that they can gain _____ from the words of

great writers and poets. And when they do their _____, they are

not worried about the _____ that the teacher gives them. They

study because they love learning something new.

4. Story Preview 🎧

Read the preview of the story. Then answer the question in *Making Predictions* on the next page.

> Knute Axelbrod is a retired farmer who decides to go to college. He is accepted at Yale University. He is excited about studying at a big university, but his love of knowledge is not enough to make him happy. The other students think he is old and strange. He becomes very lonely and disappointed and misses his farm and family.

5. Making Predictions

From the *Story Preview*, try to predict what will happen. Circle one choice below or write your own answer. Discuss your prediction with a partner.

What will Knute do at the university?

1. He will study hard and be better than the younger students.

2. He will leave the university and go back home.

3. He will go to a different university.

4. _____

6. Idioms and Expressions

You will find these idioms and expressions in the story.

---

sun went down sunset; time just before darkness

pass an examination do well on a test

boarded a train got on a train

lose its magic not be as exciting as it was before; become disappointing

don't fit in be different from other people; not belong

get there in plenty of time arrive very early

walk arm in arm walk with one arm hooked around another person's arm

get tired of become bored with something; become impatient with something

---

7. Literary Term: Setting

The *setting* is the time and place of the story. This story begins on a farm in Minnesota and ends in a university town in Connecticut. The setting changes from a peaceful landscape in the Midwest to a northeastern college town where young people from many different places come to study.

Focus As you read the story, notice how Knute's experiences change as the setting changes and how Knute feels with each experience.

About the Author

Sinclair Lewis (1885–1951), a novelist, short-story writer, and playwright, was born in Sauk Center, Minnesota. His father was a country doctor, and Sinclair often helped him when he went to visit his patients. One of his most famous novels was *Arrowsmith*, which has a country doctor as its main character.

Sinclair Lewis went to Yale University. He was a sailor, and he went to Panama to help build the Panama Canal. He had various jobs as a reporter, editor, lecturer, and writer. He published several popular novels including *Babbitt* and *Main Street*. In 1930, he became the first American to receive the Nobel Prize for Literature.

Young Man Axelbrod

Audio starts at line 113

Knute Axelbrod was born in Scandinavia. As a young man he dreamed of being a famous scholar. When he first came to America,
5 he worked all day and studied all evening. He even taught school for a short time. After he married, he gave up teaching and reading and became a farmer. He had a wife and three
10 children, and he no longer had the free time to read the books he loved.

Knute worked hard for many years. Then one day, when he was sixty-five, he realized he was an old man. His
15 wife was dead, and his children were grown up. His two sons lived in other states, and Knute decided to give the farm to his daughter Angela and her husband. He built himself a small house nearby and spent his days in 20 the garden growing vegetables and flowers.

After Knute gave his daughter his farm, he still had the habits of a farmer. He awoke at five every 25 morning, cleaned his house, made his bed, and worked in the garden. He was in bed by the time the sun went down. Soon, he began changing his habits. He slept until seven or eight in 30 the mornings, and he often took long walks at night. The neighbors began to talk about Knute. They thought his night walks were strange.

He bought a cat and named her Princess. He let her drink milk from a bowl on the kitchen table. He talked to her as if she were human.

Knute often sat in the sun and looked at the trees. His wide shoulders leaned against his rocking chair, and he touched his white beard. One day while he was sitting in his chair on the porch, he looked up at the trees and thought, "I'm an old man. I've had a good life, but there's one thing I wish for in my old age. I want to go to college. I want to be a student again and read all the great books I never had time to read."

Knute always had a young soul that looked for knowledge and beauty. He loved learning and thought that all college students loved to study and learn. He pictured Harvard and Yale as famous universities where students, like the ancient Greeks, stood around under marble temples[1] and talked about great ideas. He ordered college catalogs and textbooks. He studied Latin, algebra, English, and history. He studied twelve hours a day, and all this time he kept it a secret. Finally, one day he told his daughter.

"I just want you to know that I'm going to college. I plan to leave next week."

"Father, what are you talking about? You can't go to college. You're too old."

"I'm leaving in a few days. I'm not too old to keep learning. I've been studying, and I think I can pass the examinations."

"But the other students are eighteen or nineteen years old."

"That's not a problem. I don't have to go dancing with them. I just want to be in college with them."

"What if you get sick?"

"Angela, I'm not a child. If I get sick, I'll go to a doctor. Don't worry, my dear. I'll be all right."

Angela realized that her father was not going to listen to her. "Dad, where are you planning to go to school?"

"Yale. I'm going to Yale."

The next day he brought Princess over to his daughter's house along with some of his plants. His daughter agreed to watch his little house. Knute said goodbye and boarded a train to New Haven, Connecticut. He had to travel across the United States from his home in Minnesota.

Knute Axelbrod passed the entrance examinations and was accepted at Yale. His roommate was Ray Gribble. Ray was a teacher and wanted a degree so he could make more money. He was surprised that Knute was interested in studying literature and that he didn't care about making money.

Knute knew people at Yale thought he was strange. He listened to instructors who were younger than his sons, and his large body looked uncomfortable in the chairs in the

___

[1] *marble temples*: buildings used for religion or education and made of hard stone

classrooms. Most of the students stared at him and thought he was crazy. Soon, even Gribble, his roommate, stayed away from him.

Yale began to lose its magic for Knute. The buildings were no longer marble temples. The dining room where Knute ate his meals became a lonely place. No one sat next to him or talked to him. Several young men laughed at Knute's beard, and eventually, he began eating at a nearby restaurant. Without friends, it became harder for Knute to do his assignments. Loneliness became his friend. He missed his cat, his daughter, and his little house. He missed the walks at night and the sunshine on his porch. He had been at Yale only a month.

One day Knute climbed a large rock that overlooked the school and saw a young man sitting on a bench. It was Gil Washburn, another freshman. He was a quiet type and not very popular with the other students. Knute stared at him. The young man looked lonely, too.

Gil noticed Knute and walked over to him. "Great view," he said smiling. Knute smiled back and said, "Yes, I think The Acropolis[2] must be like this."

"You know, Knute, I've been thinking about you. We are the two who don't fit in here. We came to dream, and everyone else is here to get good grades and make money. You may not agree with me, but I think we're very much alike."

"Why do you think I came here to dream?"

"I listen to you talking in class. I watch you with the other students. Do you like poetry? I have a book I brought with me. Do you want to look at it?"

Knute took the thin, brown leather book in his big hands and touched it gently. The pages had gold on their edges. When he opened the pages, he saw a foreign language. "It's beautiful, but I can't read it."

"It's French poetry. Let me read you a little."

Gil read to Knute, and the words sounded like music. Knute had been waiting for this for sixty-five years. Then Gil said, "Listen, there's a concert in Hartford tonight, and Ysaye, a famous violinist, is playing. Let's go hear him. We'll take the train and get there in plenty of time. I asked some of the other fellows, but

---

2 *The Acropolis*: a rocky hill in the center of the city of Athens in Greece

they thought I was crazy."

Knute never heard of Ysaye, but he said, "Sure." When they got to Hartford, they found out they had just enough money to eat dinner, buy concert tickets, and pay for a train ticket to a nearby town. After the concert, Gil suggested, "Let's walk back to New Haven. Can you walk that far?" Knute had no idea how far away they were, but once again he said, "Sure."

So the young man and the older one walked beneath the October moon. They stopped to steal apples and stare at the moon. Gil did most of the talking, and Knute listened. They reached the campus at five in the morning. Knute didn't know how to thank Gil, so he said, "It was fine. I'll go to bed now and dream about our adventure."

"You can't go to bed now. The fun isn't over. Let's go get something to eat. I'm hungry. I'll go up to my room and get some money. Wait here."

Knute was delighted. He would have waited all night. He had lived sixty-five years and traveled fifteen hundred miles to find Gil Washburn. When Gil returned, the two walked arm in arm down the empty streets until they found a restaurant. For the first time, Knute felt content and happy.

They brought the food up to Gil's room. Knute sat in a comfortable chair and looked around at the books, Persian rugs, a silver tea set, and paintings. Gil started a fire in the small fireplace. As they ate, they spoke about great men and their ideas. Gil read some of his own poetry. Knute thought it was a miracle to meet someone who wrote poetry.

They began to yawn, and Knute said goodbye. As he left Gil's room, he saw the sun coming up. It was a new day.

"I can go to his room anytime now. He's my friend."

Knute held the book of French poetry, which Gil wanted him to keep. As he walked back to his own room, Knute felt very tired. In daylight, the adventure seemed hard to believe.

"Age and youth – I guess they can't be a team for long. If I saw the boy again, he would get tired of me. I told him all I know. This is what I came to college for. I waited sixty-five years for this one night. If I go away now, I won't spoil it."

He wrote a note to Gil and packed his clothes. At five that afternoon, on a westbound train, an old man sat smiling. His eyes were content, and his hands held a small book of French poetry even though he couldn't read French.

1. Understanding the Story

With a partner or in a small group, discuss the following questions.

1. Why didn't Knute go to college when he was a young man?
2. How does Knute prepare for the entrance examinations?
3. Why does Knute feel lonely?
4. Why does Knute enjoy being with Gil Washburn?
5. Why does Knute decide to leave Yale and return home?

2. Vocabulary Comprehension

The words in the list are in the story. Find the words in the story, and try to understand their meanings. Then complete the sentences with words in the list. Use each word once.

dream	soul	steal	yawn
realizes	secret	adventure	spoil
habits	stare	content	
strange	lonely	miracle	

1. Knute keeps his plan to go to college a _____*secret*_____ from his daughter.

2. Angela _____ her father won't give up his plan to go to college.

3. The other students at Yale _____ at Knute's white beard.

4. They think Knute is _____.

5. Knute doesn't have any friends at school, and he feels _____.

6. Knute thinks it is a _____ to meet someone who writes poetry.

7. When he leaves his farm in Minnesota, Knute starts a new

   _____.

8. Knute has a _____ of going to college and studying literature.

9. After Knute gives his farm to his daughter, he still has the _____

   of a farmer.

10. Knute and Gil stop to _____ apples from a tree on their walk back to Yale.

11. Knute and Gil both _____ because they are sleepy after staying up all night.

12. After spending time with Gil Washburn, Knute feels _____.

13. Knute wants to leave college so that he doesn't _____ his friendship with Gil.

14. Knute has the _____ of a scholar because he loves learning.

3. Grammar: Proper and Common Nouns

Nouns are words for people, places, or things. Most nouns are either *proper* nouns or *common* nouns.

- **Proper nouns are for *specific* people, places, or things. In English, proper nouns begin with a capital letter.**

   Specific people, places, and things include:

   names, countries, cities, states, schools, buildings, streets, rivers, lakes, oceans, nationalities, languages, religions, holidays, months, days, and titles

   Examples:

Knute Axelbrod	America	Greek
Angela	England	English
Professor Smith	Minnesota	October
Yale University	The Acropolis	Sunday

- **Common nouns are not specific people, places, or things. They do not begin with a capital letter.**

   Examples:

farmer	garden	flowers
roommate	campus	poetry
friend	temples	concert

■ *Practice 1*

In the following sentences, some proper nouns are missing. With a partner, fill in the blank lines with correct proper nouns from the story. Capitalize the first letter of each proper noun.

1. Knute Axelbrod was born in _____*Scandinavia*_____ and later came to _____*America*_____.

2. Knute had a cat named _____.

3. _____ and _____ are famous centers of learning.

4. To prepare for college, Knute studied _____, algebra, _____ and history.

5. _____ realized that her father was not going to listen to her.

6. Knute traveled by train from _____ to _____ _____, _____.

7. When Knute saw the view from the large rock, he said, "Yes, I think The _____ must be like this."

8. Knute and _____ went to a concert in _____.

9. After the concert, they walked back under the _____ moon.

10. Gil gave Knute a book of _____ poetry.

■ *Practice 2*

In the following paragraph, look for the common nouns and proper nouns. Circle the common nouns. Underline the proper nouns. Capitalize the first letter of each proper noun.

knute and gil went to hartford for a concert. They ran out of money and couldn't take a train back to yale. So they had to walk back to the university. They stayed up all night talking about great men and their ideas. In the morning, gil gave knute his book of french poetry. When knute decided to return to minnesota, he was content with his adventure in connecticut.

D | THINKING ABOUT THE STORY

1. Sharing Ideas

With a partner or in a small group, discuss the following questions.

1. Why does Knute want to go to college?
2. Why don't the younger students like Knute?
3. Compare Knute and Gil. How are they alike, and how are they different?
4. Did Knute make the right choice in returning to Minnesota? Why or why not?
5. Why do you think the story is titled "Young Man Axelbrod"?

2. Reading Between the Lines

Authors often write something that can have more than one meaning. You need to figure out what the author means. This is called *reading between the lines*. Read the following sentences from the story. Then circle the answer that shows the author's meaning. If you need help, look back at the story. Discuss your answers.

1. Knute always had a young soul that looked for knowledge and beauty.

    a. Knute was a young man.

    b. Knute wanted to keep on learning even though he was older.

    c. Knute loved beautiful clothes and jewelry.

2. Most of the students stared at Knute and thought he was crazy.

    a. Most students were scared of Knute because he was big.

    b. Most students didn't like Knute because he had an unusual name.

    c. Most students thought Knute was too old, too big, and too strange.

3. Yale began to lose its magic for Knute.

    a. Yale was not the wonderful place Knute thought it would be.

    b. Yale didn't teach magic.

    c. Knute wanted to become young again.

3. Analyzing the Story: Setting

As you read on page 6, the *setting* is the time and place of the story. In this story, there are several settings. Knute has different experiences and feelings in each setting. Choose the correct experiences and feelings to complete the chart.

Experiences
- The other students don't sit next to Knute or talk to him.
- Knute thinks about his adventures.
- Gil reads his poetry.
- Knute and Gil walk and talk beneath the October moon.

Feelings
- Knute has a good time, but he doesn't know how to thank Gil.
- Knute is content.
- Knute is lonely and disappointed.
- Knute thinks it is a miracle to meet someone who writes poetry.

SETTING	EXPERIENCES	FEELINGS
In the classrooms and dining room at Yale		*Knute is lonely and disappointed.*
On the road from Hartford to New Haven		
In Gil Washburn's room		
On a train to Minnesota	*Knute thinks about his adventures.*	

4. Summary

Put the following sentences in the correct order to summarize the story. Write the numbers 1 to 7 to show the order. The first one has been done for you.

_____ Knute takes an examination and is accepted at Yale.

_____ Gil gives Knute a book of French poetry.

_____ Knute feels lonely at school.

_____ Knute meets Gil Washburn, who becomes his friend.

___1___ Knute decides to go to college.

_____ Knute and Gil go to a concert and stay up all night.

_____ Knute decides to return to Minnesota.

5. Writing

Pretend you are Knute. Write a letter to Gil telling him why you left Yale.

Chapter 2

A Pair of Silk Stockings KATE CHOPIN

A PRE-READING

1. Think Before You Read

Answer the following questions.

1. What are the qualities of a good mother? List them.
2. Why do people save money? What things do they usually save their money to buy?
3. Do you like to buy things for yourself or for other people? Explain your answer.

2. Picture Focus

With a partner, talk about the picture.

What do you think the woman is thinking about? How do you think she feels?

3. Key Vocabulary

Study the following key words from the story. They all relate to *shopping* and *money*. Then complete the paragraph using each word once.

---

save keep your money, not spend it

wallet something to carry and keep money in

bargain something that is sold at a very good price – much lower than usual

sale a time when things in a store are sold at a special low price

reduced at a lower price than is normal

change the money you get back when you give more money than the cost of something

---

Everyone likes to get a _____. When a store has a big

_____, a lot of people will come to shop. They will look for things

that are _____. It's great to get something for less money than it

usually costs. Then you can put the _____ in your

_____ and _____ it for another day.

4. Story Preview 🎧

Read the preview of the story. Then answer the question in *Making Predictions* on the next page.

> Mrs. Sommers is a housewife in the late 1800s. She is usually very practical. She always saves her money and thinks carefully about how to spend it. One day she goes shopping by herself. She has $15 and plans to buy new clothes for her four children.

5. Making Predictions

From the *Story Preview*, try to predict what will happen. Circle one choice below or write your own answer. Discuss your prediction with a partner.

What will Mrs. Sommers do when she goes shopping with her $15?

1. She will buy new clothes for her children.

2. She will spend the money on herself.

3. She will save the money and add more money to it.

4. _____

6. Idioms and Expressions

You will find these idioms and expressions in the story.

watched every penny spent money carefully
better days a time in the past when life was easier
on sale selling at a lower price
May I help you? a polite way of asking someone if he or she needs assistance
I'll take this. I'll buy this.
took a seat sat down

7. Literary Term: Sensory Details

Writers use *sensory details* to create images of the five senses – *touch*, *taste*, *smell*, *sight*, and *sound*. For example, to create the image of touching, the author of this story wrote, ". . . her hand was touching something very soft and pleasant." To create the image of tasting, she wrote, "She closed her eyes and remembered the delicious lunch."

Focus   As you read the story, notice the sensory details the author uses to create images. Do they help you see, hear, touch, smell, or taste?

About the Author

Kate Chopin (1851–1904) was born Katherine O'Flaherty in St. Louis, Missouri. Her father was born in Ireland, but he had a very successful business in St. Louis. He died when Chopin was very young. Her mother was French Creole,[1] and Chopin was very close to her mother and to her French-speaking grandmother. Chopin had a very interesting life as a child. She spoke both French and English, played the piano, and read many books.

As an adult, Chopin was admired for her independence and intelligence. She married Oscar Chopin, moved to New Orleans, and had six children. However, she wasn't a typical housewife of the late 1800s. When her husband died suddenly, she didn't have any money. She began earning money by writing short stories.

Kate Chopin was one of America's favorite short story writers of her time and is still very popular. Most of her stories deal with women who have difficult lives and who want to be independent.

A Pair of Silk Stockings

Audio starts at line 37

Mrs. Sommers was amazed to discover that the money she saved every week was now $15. This was a large amount for someone who watched every penny and was so careful with money. She smiled as she touched her wallet with a feeling of pride.

Life was easier years ago. Those were "better days," but now she couldn't think about the past. She was too busy taking care of her family and spending every dollar carefully. Now she had $15 in her wallet!

For several days she walked around

[1] *Creole*: in North America, a person who is a mixture of Native American, French, Spanish, European, African, or Caribbean

thinking about how to spend her treasure. During the quiet hours at night when the children were asleep, she stayed awake making plans to spend the money.

Perhaps she could spend a dollar more on Janie's shoes, and she could buy Mag a dress. She could buy material to make new shirts for the boys. She could get caps for the boys and hats for the girls. The thought of her four children dressed in new clothes made her excited and happy.

Mrs. Sommers knew the value of bargains. She could stand on line for hours waiting to buy something on sale. She always tried to get the lowest price. But this day she was a little tired. After feeding the children and sending them off to school, she went out on a shopping trip. She was in such a hurry, she forgot to eat lunch.

After entering the department store, Mrs. Sommers stood in front of a counter. She put her hand down on the counter to rest for a few minutes. Suddenly, she realized that her hand was touching something very soft and pleasant. She looked down and saw that her hand was lying on some silk stockings. The sign nearby said the stockings were reduced from $2.50 to $1.98.

A young saleswoman asked, "May I help you choose some silk stockings?"

Mrs. Sommers smiled and stared at the stockings as if they were jewels. She began to blush, "Do you have any stockings in size eight?"

"Oh, yes. What color do you want?" replied the saleswoman. "We have light blue, tan, gray, and black.

"I would like the black, please."

When the saleswoman brought her the stockings, Mrs. Sommers looked at them for a long time. "I'll take this pair," she said. She handed the woman a five-dollar bill and held her hand out waiting for the change and the package. It was such a small package. It seemed to disappear when she dropped it into her old shopping bag.

Then Mrs. Sommers took the elevator to the Ladies Room on the top floor. Here in a corner, she took off her cotton stockings and put on the new silk ones. She was no longer thinking in the practical way she usually did. She was not thinking at all. The silk felt so wonderful on her skin. She leaned back in the soft chair and enjoyed the feeling of luxury. Then she put on her shoes and walked straight to the shoe department.

The clerk spent a lot of time bringing her shoes to try on. Finally, she chose a pair which she wore immediately. Her next stop was the glove department where she chose a pair of black leather gloves with small pearl buttons at the wrists.

Mrs. Sommers felt very happy, and she walked with her head high and a small smile on her face. She felt pretty and young again. She also felt very hungry. Then she noticed a restaurant she had never been in. She entered and was seated at a table by herself. She ordered a shrimp cocktail and a glass of wine. For dessert she had black coffee with a slice of chocolate cake. The restaurant was very pleasant. Other people were quietly eating and talking. There was soft music playing, and a breeze blew in from the windows. When she paid her bill, she added a generous tip for the waiter. He bowed as she left as if she were a princess.

There was still money in her wallet. Her next luxury was going to see a play. She walked into the theater and sat down just as the play was starting. As the curtain rose, Mrs. Sommers sat back in her seat and smiled. She laughed at the funny moments and cried at the sad ones. When the play ended and the music stopped, Mrs. Sommers sat in her seat a little longer. She was the last one to leave the theater.

Mrs. Sommers waited for the bus on the corner. She climbed onto the bus and took a seat behind the driver. She was no longer smiling. She began to think about all the things she had to do at home. Then she remembered her wonderful day. She touched the silk stockings on her legs. She unbuttoned her soft

> *Mrs. Sommers felt very happy, and she walked with her head high and a small smile on her face. She felt pretty and young again.*

leather gloves. She closed her eyes and remembered the delicious lunch. Then she remembered sitting in the theater and watching the play. Deep in her heart there was a powerful wish. She wished the bus driver would keep driving on and on and never stop. She wanted this day to last forever.

1. Understanding the Story

With a partner or in a small group, discuss the following questions.

1. How does Mrs. Sommers plan to spend the $15 before she goes shopping?
2. What does she actually buy when she goes on her shopping trip?
3. Where does Mrs. Sommers go after she is finished shopping?
4. Why is Mrs. Sommers the last one to leave the theater?
5. Why does she want the bus driver to keep driving forever?

2. Vocabulary Comprehension

The words in the list are in the word search box. Find the words in the box. The words are written across or down. After you have found the words, use them to complete the sentences. Use each word only once.

amazed	treasure	generous	blushed
wished	pleasant	bowed	luxury
pride	practical	stared	leaned

```
A B D P P R I D E S B Y D I T C R L S X L
Y L T R E A S U R E L B E S W X C O M Q E
B L U S H E D R N W U A Q T J C W T D R A
O U Z A M A Z E D G X P R A C T I C A L N
W X T A G E N E R O U S I R Z A G K O Y E
E U R H W K P I B N R P L E A S A N T Q D
D R W I S H E D X C Y U V D D L F H W K Z
```

1. Mrs. Sommers thought the money she saved was a _____treasure_____.

2. She was _____ to find out she had saved $15.

3. She also had a feeling of _____ because she saved so much money.

4. When Mrs. Sommers went to the department store, she _____

   on the counter and felt something soft.

5. The stockings felt _____ .

6. Mrs. Sommers _____ at the stockings as if they were jewels.

7. Mrs. Sommers _____ when she asked for a pair of stockings.

8. Mrs. Sommers prided herself on being _____ about spending money.

9. Although the silk stockings were a _____ , they were on sale.

10. Mrs. Sommers gave the waiter a _____ tip.

11. He _____ to her as if she were a princess.

12. Mrs. Sommers _____ that her day of luxury would last forever.

3. *Grammar: Adjectives*

Adjectives are words that describe nouns and pronouns. Nouns can also serve as adjectives when they describe other nouns. Without adjectives our writing would be very boring.

In English, adjectives are usually placed before nouns. An adjective helps us imagine what a place, person, or thing looks like. In the example below, you can see how the adjectives can create a very different picture of a person or a place.

Examples:
A tall, thin, black-haired man walked into a small, dark, ugly room.
A short, fat, fair-haired man walked into a large, lovely, sunlit room.

When a sentence has a *be* verb (*is, am, are, was,* or *were*) or a linking verb (*feel, look, smell, taste, sound, become, seem,* etc.), the noun can come before the verb, and the adjective can come after the verb. Think of the linking verb as an equal sign (=).

Examples:
The stockings are beautiful.
The gloves feel soft.

■ *Practice 1*

This story uses many adjectives that help us imagine Mrs. Sommers and the experiences she has in one day. Find the adjectives in the following sentences and underline them. Then circle the nouns they describe.

1. Mrs. Sommers bought a pair of <u>soft</u>, <u>black</u> <u>leather</u> (gloves.)

2. The gloves had small, pearl buttons at the wrists.

3. She felt like a pretty, young woman again.

4. It was a small package.

5. There was soft music playing.

6. In the theater, she laughed at the funny moments and cried at the sad ones.

7. Then she remembered her wonderful day.

8. Deep in her heart there was a powerful wish.

■ *Practice 2*

In the following sentences, underline the adjectives and circle the nouns or pronouns they describe.

1. Mrs. Sommers is good, caring, and careful with money.

2. The silk felt wonderful on her skin.

3. The gloves felt soft, and they looked beautiful.

4. She felt pretty and young again.

5. She also became very hungry.

6. The coffee and cake tasted delicious.

7. Mrs. Sommers seemed happy buying luxuries for herself.

8. Mrs. Sommers became sad when she rode the bus home.

1. Sharing Ideas

With a partner or in a small group, discuss the following questions.

1. Why does Mrs. Sommers change her plan to buy clothes for her children?
2. Why does Mrs. Sommers blush when she talks to the saleswoman?
3. Do you think it is good that Mrs. Sommers spent all the money on herself? Why or why not?
4. Do you think Mrs. Sommers is sad when she returns home?
5. Have you ever spent a lot of money on yourself? What did you do? How did you feel after you spent the money?

2. Reading Between the Lines

Authors often write something that can have more than one meaning. You need to figure out what the author means. This is called *reading between the lines*. Read the following sentences from the story. Then circle the answer that shows the author's meaning. If you need help, look back at the story. Discuss your answers.

1. Mrs. Sommers smiled and stared at the stockings as if they were jewels.

   a. Mrs. Sommers really wanted jewelry.

   b. She thought the stockings looked very beautiful.

   c. The stockings cost as much as jewels.

2. It was such a small package. It seemed to disappear when she dropped it into her old shopping bag.

   a. The shopping bag was too big and too old to carry pretty silk stockings.

   b. It was easy for Mrs. Sommers to forget that she had bought herself something valuable because the package was so small.

   c. It was going to be difficult for Mrs. Sommers to find the package again in her large shopping bag.

3. She felt pretty and young again.

   a. She wished she did not have children so she could have more fun.

   b. She felt men were looking at her and noticing her.

   c. She enjoyed buying new things and taking care of herself.

4. She wanted this day to last forever.

    a. Mrs. Sommers didn't want to see her children again.

    b. Mrs. Sommers felt bad because the next day she would have no money.

    c. Mrs. Sommers didn't want the day to end because she was enjoying herself.

3. Analyzing the Story: Sensory Details

As you read on page 18, authors use *sensory details* to help you imagine the five senses. The items listed below are from the story. Put them in the correct rows to complete the chart. Some items may go in more than one row.

1. staring at the stockings
2. listening to the music in the restaurant
3. drinking wine
4. watching the play
5. resting her hand on the counter
6. eating a shrimp cocktail
7. feeling the silk stockings on her legs
8. unbuttoning her leather gloves
9. drinking black coffee
10. feeling the breeze through the open window

TOUCH	
TASTE	
SMELL	
SIGHT	*staring at the stockings*
SOUND	

Did the author help you imagine Mrs. Sommers's day? Discuss your answer with a partner.

4. Summary

Put the following sentences in the correct order to summarize the story. Write the numbers 1 to 6 to show the order. The first one has been done for you.

_____ She takes a bus back to her home and is sorry the day is over.

_____ She has lunch in a pleasant restaurant.

_____ Mrs. Sommers buys a pair of black silk stockings.

_____ Mrs. Sommers goes to the theater to see a play.

_____ She buys a pair of shoes and some gloves.

___1___ Mrs. Sommers, who is careful about spending money, saves $15.

5. Writing

Pretend you are Mrs. Sommers. Write in your diary about the day you spent in town. Describe what you did. Answer the following questions and try to use sensory details.

Where did you go?

What did you do?

How did you feel?

Chapter 3
One Thousand Dollars O. Henry

A PRE-READING

1. Think Before You Read

Answer the following questions.

1. What would you do if someone gave you $1,000? Would you spend it, save it, or give it away?
2. Have you ever given money to someone? How did it make you feel?
3. Can money make you happy? Why or why not?

2. Picture Focus

With a partner, talk about the picture.

Who are these men? Why do you think one man is giving money to another?

3. Key Vocabulary

Study the following key words from the story. They all relate to *money or property when someone dies*. Then complete the paragraph using each word once.

---

lawyer someone who gives legal advice

will a written statement of who should get your money or property when you die

deceased a formal way of describing someone who is no longer living; dead

leave give something to someone after you die

inherit receive money or property from someone who has died

heirs people who receive money or property from someone who has died

---

As you get older, it is important that you write a _____. This statement will say who will _____ your money or property when you are _____. Before you write it, you should go to a _____ to get advice. Normally, people _____ their money or property to their relatives. But your _____ don't have to be your relatives. You can also give your money to your favorite charity or your cat!

4. Story Preview 🎧

Read the preview of the story. Then answer the question in *Making Predictions* on the next page.

Bob Gillian has just received $1,000 from his uncle's will. He has to spend the money and then tell his uncle's lawyers how he spent it. If he can prove that he used the $1,000 wisely and unselfishly, he will get an additional $50,000. Otherwise, another person will inherit the money.

5. Making Predictions

From the *Story Preview*, try to predict what will happen. Circle one choice below or write your own answer. Discuss your prediction with a partner.

How will Bob Gillian spend the $1,000?

1. He will spend it on a girlfriend.

2. He will lose it.

3. He will give it away.

4. _____

6. Idioms and Expressions

You will find these idioms and expressions in the story.

paid attention to listened carefully to someone or something

be worth be equal in value to

depend on need the support of someone or something

go on stage appear in a play in a theater

Would you mind . . . ? a polite way to ask for something

turned white became scared

7. Literary Term: Character

The people in a story are called *characters*. The most important people in a story are the *main* characters. Other people in the story are *minor* characters. Good writers make you understand the people in their stories. You understand why they do things and how they feel.

Focus As you read this story, decide who the main character is. How do you feel about this character? Does the main character surprise you at the end of the story?

About the Author

O. Henry (1862–1910) was born William Sydney Porter in Greensboro, North Carolina. When he was a young man, he moved to Texas where he married and worked in a bank.

However, Porter was extremely unlucky in Texas. His young wife was sick, and he was accused of stealing money from the bank. He ran away to Honduras in Central America, but he returned to the United States when he learned that his wife was dying. After her death in 1897, Porter was found guilty and sent to jail for five years. While he was in prison, Porter wrote and sold at least 12 stories and changed his name to O. Henry. When he was released from jail, he moved to New York and wrote for many magazines.

One Thousand Dollars

Audio starts at line 22

"What can I do with a thousand dollars?"

"One thousand dollars," repeated Lawyer Tolman, seriously, "and here is the money."

Young Bob Gillian laughed as he picked up the thin package of new fifty-dollar bills. "It's such a difficult amount of money. It's too much to spend and too little to invest," he said. "I'll have to think about it."

Lawyer Tolman said, "You heard the reading of your uncle's will. I do not know if you paid much attention to its details. I want to remind you of one detail. You have to tell us how you spent this $1,000. The will states that clearly. So, I hope you will do as your uncle wished.

"I'll do my best," said the young man politely.

Gillian went to his club. There he looked for his friend Bryson. He found him in a corner reading a book. Gillian interrupted him. "I have a funny story to tell you," he said. "I just came from my deceased uncle's company. He left me one thousand dollars. Now, what can I do with a thousand dollars?"

"I thought," said Bryson, "that your deceased uncle was worth something like half a million."

"He was," answered Gillian, "and that's where the joke comes in. He left his whole fortune to science. The butler and the housekeeper get $10 each. I inherited $1,000."

"Well, you don't have to worry. You've always had plenty of money to spend," said Bryson.

"That's true," Gillian said. "Uncle always gave me money when I asked for it."

"Are there any other heirs?" Bryson asked.

"None," Bob Gillian looked upset. "There is a Miss Hayden, my uncle's secretary, who lived in his house. She's a quiet woman – musical – the daughter of a friend. I forgot to say she got $10 also. But tell me, what can I do with a thousand dollars?"

"You?" said Bryson with a laugh. "You can buy Miss Lotta Lauriere a diamond necklace with the money."

"Thanks," said Gillian, rising. "I thought I could depend on you, Bryson."

Gillian phoned for a cab and said to the driver, "Take me to the stage entrance of the Columbine Theatre."

Miss Lotta Lauriere was putting on makeup in her dressing room when Gillian knocked on the door.

"Come in," said Miss Lauriere. "Oh, it's you, Bobbie. I don't have much time. I go on stage in two minutes."

"It won't take me two minutes, Lotta. How would you like a diamond necklace? I have a thousand dollars."

"Only a thousand?" she asked. "If you can get me the necklace I saw in Tiffany's for three thousand, then I'll be interested."

Gillian opened the door and walked out. He got into a taxi and said to the driver, "Drive until I tell you to stop."

Eight blocks down Broadway, Gillian got out. A blind man on the sidewalk was selling pencils. Gillian stood in front of him and said, "Excuse me, but would you mind telling me what you would do if you had a thousand dollars?"

The blind man answered, "I'm not sure I need a thousand dollars. Here, take a look at this if you like." The blind man took a bank book out of his coat pocket. Gillian opened it. It showed a balance of $1,785 to the blind man's credit.

Gillian returned the book and got into the cab. He told the driver, "Take me to the law offices of Tolman and Sharpe at 1740 Broadway."

When he entered the office, Mr. Tolman looked at him in an unfriendly way. "May I ask you a question?" Gillian said, "Was Miss Hayden left anything in my uncle's will besides $10?"

"Nothing," said the lawyer.

"I thank you very much, Sir," Gillian said, and he went out to his cab. He gave the driver the address of his uncle's home.

Miss Hayden was writing letters. She was small and thin and dressed in black. Gillian greeted her and said, "I've just come from Tolman's office. They've been looking at some papers and found that my uncle left you a thousand dollars. Here it is." Gillian laid the money on the desk.

Miss Hayden turned white. "Oh," she said, and again, "Oh."

Gillian half turned and looked out of the window. "I suppose, of course," he said in a low voice, "that you know I love you."

"I'm sorry," said Miss Hayden, taking the money.

"I guess there is no chance that you feel the same about me?" Gillian asked.

"No, I'm very sorry," she repeated.

"May I write a note?" Gillian asked with a smile. He seated himself at a big table. She gave him paper and a pen, and then quietly went back to her desk.

Gillian wrote how he spent the thousand dollars in these words: "One thousand dollars to the best and dearest woman on earth." He put the note into an envelope and left.

His cab stopped again at the office of Tolman and Sharp.

"I have spent the thousand dollars," Gillian told Mr. Tolman, "and I have come to give you a written report." He laid it on the desk as Tolman opened the door of the safe and called his partner, Sharp.

They took a large envelope out of the safe and Mr. Tolman said, "There is an addition to your uncle's will. It states that if you spent the thousand dollars wisely and unselfishly, you will receive $50,000. If not, Miriam Hayden will get the money."

Tolman reached for the envelope, but Gillian tore it up and said, "You don't need to read this. I'll tell you. I lost the thousand dollars betting on a horse at the race track. Good afternoon, Gentlemen."

Tolman and Sharp shook their heads sadly at each other when Bob Gillian left, for they heard him whistling happily as he waited for the elevator.

1. Understanding the Story

With a partner or in a small group, discuss the following questions.

1. What advice does Bryson give Gillian?
2. Why does Lotta Lauriere refuse Gillian's offer to buy her a diamond necklace?
3. Why doesn't Gillian give the $1,000 to the blind man?
4. How does Gillian finally spend the $1,000?
5. Why does Gillian tear up his note to the lawyers?

2. Vocabulary Comprehension

The words in the list are in the story. Read the sentences below from the story. Then circle the letter of the best meaning of the **bold** word in each sentence.

seriously	remind	joke	addition
invest	politely	fortune	unselfishly
details	interrupt	balance	whistling

1. "One thousand dollars," repeated Lawyer Tolman, **seriously**, . . .
   a. jokingly
   b. without humor
   c. in an unfriendly manner

2. "It's too much to spend and too little to **invest**."
   a. put in the bank
   b. give away
   c. buy something to make more money

3. "I do not know if you paid much attention to its **details**."
   a. description
   b. summaries
   c. specific facts and information

4. "I want to **remind** you of one detail."
   a. help someone remember
   b. help someone review
   c. help someone change

5. "I'll do my best," said the young man **politely**.
   a. with good manners
   b. carelessly
   c. without paying attention

6. He found him in a corner reading a book. Gillian **interrupted** him.
   a. woke him up
   b. stopped him from what he was doing
   c. shouted at him

7. ". . . that's where the **joke** comes in."
   a. the funny thing
   b. mistake
   c. trick

8. "He left his whole **fortune** to science."
   a. future earnings
   b. large amount of money, possessions, or property
   c. bank account

9. The blind man took a bank book out of his coat pocket. . . . It showed a **balance** of $1,785 . . . .
   a. amount of money a person has
   b. amount of money owed
   c. amount of money spent

10. "There is an **addition** to your uncle's will."
    a. change
    b. new item
    c. mistake

11. "It states that if you spent the money wisely and **unselfishly**, you will receive $50,000."
    a. foolishly
    b. caring about others
    c. intelligently

12. . . . they heard him **whistling** happily as he waited for the elevator.
    a. singing
    b. making a musical sound with his lips
    c. humming

3. Grammar: Adverbs

Adverbs are words that modify (describe, change, or add information to) action verbs, adjectives, and other adverbs. Adverbs also answer the questions of *where, when, how, how much.*

> **Adverbs modify verbs.** In the following sentence from the story, *seriously* is an adverb because it modifies the verb *repeated.* The adverb here answers the question *how.*
>
> "One thousand dollars," repeated Lawyer Tolman, seriously . . . .

> **Adverbs modify adjectives.** In this sentence from the story, *too* modifies the adjective *little.* The adverb here answers the question *how much.*
>
> "It's . . . too little to invest."

> **Adverbs modify other adverbs.** In this sentence from the story, *very* modifies the adverb *much.*
>
> "I thank you very much, Sir."

> **You will find that many adverbs add *-ly* to the adjective form. However, not all words that end in *-ly* are adverbs. In this sentence from the story, *unfriendly* is an adjective (not an adverb) that modifies *way.*
>
> Mr. Tolman looked at him in an unfriendly way.

> **Some adverbs do not have an adjective form. Examples are *just, always, then, again, soon, not, very,* and *never.*

■ *Practice 1*

In each of the following sentences from the story, there is at least one adverb. Find the adverb and underline it. Then in the space on the right, write the word the adverb modifies.

1. "I'll do my best," said the young man <u>politely</u>.   *said*

2. "I just came from my deceased uncle's company."   _____

3. "You've always had plenty of money to spend."   _____

4. She gave him paper and a pen, and then quietly went

   back to her desk. _____

5. His cab stopped again at the office of Tolman and Sharp. _____

6. "It states that if you spent the thousand dollars wisely and

   unselfishly, you will receive $50,000." _____

7. Tolman and Sharp shook their heads sadly . . . . _____

8. . . . they heard him whistling happily as he waited for

   the elevator. _____

■ *Practice 2*

Look at the list of adverbs and adjectives below. Complete the sentences in the paragraph with words from the list. Then put *1* above the adverbs and *2* above the adjectives. Use each word once.

selfishly	bad	careful	carelessly	many
only	politely	serious	very	wisely

The young man listened ___*politely*___¹ to his lawyer. His lawyer read him

a will from his uncle. The lawyer was _____ _____

as he read the will. There were _____ details. The young man paid

_____ attention to the details. His uncle was leaving him one

thousand dollars. At first, he would get _____ half of the money. If

he spent it _____, he would get the other half. If he spent it

_____ or _____, he would not get the other half.

The young man thought his uncle's will was a _____ joke.

1. *Sharing Ideas*

With a partner or in a small group, discuss the following questions.

1. Why doesn't Miss Hayden return Gillian's love?
2. Does Gillian really love Miss Hayden, or does he love Miss Lauriere?
3. What would happen if Gillian did not tear up his note?
4. What do you think Miss Hayden will do with the money?
5. What would you do if you were Gillian?

2. *Reading Between the Lines*

Authors often write something that can have more than one meaning. You need to figure out what the author means. This is called *reading between the lines*. Read the following sentences from the story. Then circle the answer that shows the author's meaning. If you need help, look back at the story. Discuss your answers.

1. ". . . and that's where the joke comes in. He left his whole fortune to science."
   a. Gillian thinks his uncle was a funny man.
   b. Gillian can't believe his uncle left all his money only to science.
   c. Gillian is telling his friend a lie.

2. Gillian said, "Was Miss Hayden left anything in my uncle's will besides $10?"
   a. Gillian is thinking of giving his money to Miss Hayden.
   b. Gillian wants Miss Hayden's money.
   c. Gillian wants to know if Miss Hayden got his uncle's house.

3. "I've just come from Tolman's office. They've been looking at some papers and found that my uncle left you a thousand dollars. Here it is."
   a. Gillian wants Miss Hayden to have the one thousand dollars.
   b. Gillian is joking with Miss Hayden.
   c. Gillian is telling Miss Hayden that the lawyers made a mistake.

4. "I'm sorry," said Miss Hayden, taking the money.

   a. She doesn't believe Gillian really loves her.

   b. She is being polite.

   c. She doesn't love Gillian.

5. Tolman and Sharp shook their heads sadly at each other when Bob Gillian left, for they heard him whistling happily as he waited for the elevator.

   a. Tolman and Sharp don't understand why Gillian is happy after losing the $50,000.

   b. Tolman and Sharp think Gillian made the right decision.

   c. Tolman and Sharp are sad that Gillian's uncle died.

3. Analyzing the Story: Character

As you read on page 30, good writers help you understand the *characters* in their stories. The chart below has the names of characters in the story. Complete the chart. Add adjectives that describe each character. (Find some adjectives on pages 22–24 in Chapter 2.) Add adverbs to complete the phrases. (Find some adverbs on pages 34, 36, and 37 of this chapter.)

CHARACTERS	ADJECTIVES	ADVERBS
Bob Gillian	*pleasant*	spends money
Lawyer Tolman		shook his head
Lotta Lauriere	*busy*	speaks _____ *quickly*
Miss Hayden		talks _____
Bryson		listens _____ *carefully*

4. Summary

Put the following sentences in the correct order to summarize the story. Write the numbers 1 to 7 to show the order. The first one has been done for you.

_____ Gillian writes a note and later tears it up.

_____ Miss Lotta Lauriere refuses Gillian's offer to buy her a diamond necklace.

_____ Gillian's inheritance will be given to Miss Hayden.

_____ Gillian gives the $1,000 to Miss Hayden.

___1___ In his will, Gillian's uncle gives Gillian $1,000.

_____ Gillian has to tell how he spent the $1,000.

_____ Gillian asks a blind man how he would spend $1,000.

5. Writing

Describe Miss Hayden's life a year after she received the $50,000.

Summing Up

A TAKE A CLOSER LOOK

1. Theme Comparison: Making Choices

Making choices is a theme in all the stories in Part One. Knute Axelbrod decided to go to college later in his life. Mrs. Sommers decided to spend money on herself. Bob Gillian unselfishly decided to give up a $50,000 inheritance.

With a partner, discuss the following questions.

1. Before the three main characters of the stories made their decisions, what were their choices?
2. How did the three characters make their choices? Did anyone help them?
3. Were the three characters happy with their final choices?

2. Freewriting

Write the words *making choices* at the top of a sheet of paper. Then write any words that come into your mind when you think of *making choices*. For 15 minutes, write about a time in your life when you had to make an important choice. What was the situation? What were your choices? What was your final choice? How did you make your choice?

B REVIEW

1. Grammar Review

Read the following paragraph. Underline all the nouns, circle all the adjectives, and box all the adverbs.

In the (first) story you read, Knute Axelbrod made a [very] (unusual) decision. He decided to go to college, but he was very lonely. He made only one friend, Gil. He and Gil spent one enjoyable evening together. They talked about poetry. In the second story, Mrs. Sommers bought a pair of silk stockings. She also had lunch in an expensive restaurant. Then she saw a wonderful play in the theater. In the final story, Gillian gave away his inheritance to the small, quiet secretary of his uncle. He told the two lawyers he spent the money foolishly on a horse race.

2. Vocabulary Review

Discover the vocabulary words by filling in the missing letters. Meanings are given after each word. If you need help, look back at the three stories you read in Part One.

1. a __ d __ __ __ __ __   something added on

2. a __ v __ __ __ __ __ e   an exciting trip or experience

3. a __ __ z __ __   surprised, filled with wonder

4. b __ l __ __ c __   what is left over

5. b l __ __ __   pink color in the face, usually when embarrassed

6. b __ w __ __   bent over to show respect or to say thank you

7. l __ __ n __ __   rested on, such as a hand on a table

8. l __ __ __ l y   feeling sad; being alone

9. l __ x __ __ y   something one doesn't need but wants

10. p __ __ __ s __ __ __   nice

11. p __ l __ __ __ __ y   using good manners

12. p __ __ c __ __ __ __ l   useful

13. p __ __ d __   feeling of worth

14. s __ r __ __ __ s __ y   without humor

15. s __ __ l   spirit, essence of a person

16. s __ __ r __   look at something for a long time

17. s t __ __ __   take something that doesn't belong to you

18. s __ r __ __ g __   unusual; odd; unfamiliar

Filling Out the Elements Chart

This chart shows the five basic elements of a short story. You can find definitions for these elements on page 170. Some of these elements have been filled out for "Young Man Axelbrod." Complete the chart. Then copy the blank chart on page xvii and fill it out for "A Pair of Silk Stockings" or "One Thousand Dollars" or for both stories. Share your charts with a partner or in a small group.

Elements of _____ Young Man Axelbrod _____
(name of story)

SETTING

CHARACTERS

PLOT
Knute Axelbrod is a retired farmer who wants to be a scholar. He decides to go to college and gets accepted at Yale University. At Yale he becomes lonely and disappointed because the other students think he is strange. Then he meets Gil Washburn, another freshman. One night they go to a music concert, walk in the moonlight, and discuss great men and their ideas. Gil reads a book of French poetry to Knute and then gives it to him. Knute is content, but the next morning he decides to return home to his farm.

CONFLICT
The conflict is between Knute's desire to become a serious student and the difficulty he faces because he is no longer young and is different from the other students.

THEME(S)
Sometimes our dreams and plans don't happen the way we want them to. One wonderful experience can make up for many disappointments.

The Role of Fate

WE OFTEN HEAR a happy couple say on their wedding day, "It was fate that brought us together." Fate, or destiny, is defined as something that happens to us, good or bad, that we cannot change or control. Some people believe this is true. Other people think we are free to make choices and control our own fate. Writers often use the role of fate in literature.

In the first story you are about to read, a force of nature changes the lives of all the characters. In the second story, the main character is unaware of events that happen to him while he is sleeping. In the final story, a young couple fall in love, and the woman's father tries to end their relationship. As you read these stories, ask yourself if any of the characters have control of their own fate.

Chapter 6

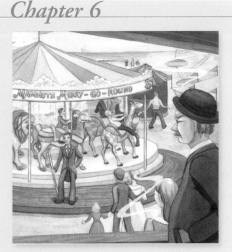

THE PACE OF YOUTH
– *Stephen Crane*

Chapter 4
The Luck of Roaring Camp BRET HARTE

A PRE-READING

1. Think Before You Read

Answer the following questions.

1. What was discovered in California in 1849 that made some people very rich?
2. What type of men do you think became rich from this discovery? What was their life like before they became rich? Was it easy or difficult?
3. Do you think these types of men could take care of a baby? Why or why not?

2. Picture Focus

With a partner, talk about the picture.

Why do you think there is a baby but no woman in the picture?

3. Key Vocabulary

Study the following key words and expressions from the story. They all relate to *luck*. Then complete the paragraph using each word or expression once.

> **gamble** something you do when you take a chance or try to be lucky
>
> **bet** tell someone what you think will happen in the future, and usually ask for money if you are correct
>
> **hope** belief that something good may happen
>
> **lucky charms** objects that people believe will bring them good luck; a rabbit's foot is one type of lucky charm
>
> **fortunate** lucky

In the mid-nineteenth century, people from all over the world went to the American West looking for gold. These people, usually men, left their homes with the _____ that they would find gold. They _____ their friends and families that they would come home rich. Some men carried special objects with them to bring them luck. These objects are called _____ _____. Unfortunately, they didn't help most of the men. Finding gold was a big _____. The men worked for days, weeks, or months, but only a few were _____ enough to find gold and return home rich.

4. Story Preview 🎧

Read the preview of the story. Then answer the question in *Making Predictions* on the next page.

> There are a hundred men and one woman in Roaring Camp. They have all come to look for gold. The woman dies giving birth to a baby boy. At first the men don't know what to do with the baby. Then they adopt him and call him "The Luck."

5. Making Predictions

From the *Story Preview*, try to predict what will happen. Circle one choice below or write your own answer. Discuss your prediction with a partner.

What will happen to The Luck?

1. One of the men will get married so The Luck will have a mother.

2. The men will find a family for him.

3. The Luck will be very happy with so many men to take care of him.

4. _____

6. Idioms and Expressions

You will find these idioms and expressions in the story.

giving birth having a baby

showed no sign of hid a true feeling or action

pull through continue to live or succeed after a hard time

one by one one person or thing following behind another

take a close look at look at something carefully

brought good luck helped someone have good luck

a great deal of a lot of

7. Literary Term: Local Color

Local color is anything in the story that helps give the reader a clear picture of what the life and times of the story were like. It may describe the people's clothing, actions, or speech. It may describe the scenery's buildings, landscape, or weather. In this story, local color describes the men of a western mining town in the nineteenth century.

Focus As you read the story, notice the actions of the men and the words they use to talk to each other. Notice the things the men have. Notice the descriptions of the weather and the landscape.

About the Author

Bret Harte (1836–1902) was born in Albany, New York. He lived an exciting life. He worked in many different jobs. He was a newspaper reporter, taught school, and became an editor, in San Francisco and Boston. He represented the United States as a consul in Germany and in Scotland. Harte also wrote poems, a novel, and some plays.

When he was a young man, Harte went to the American West to look for gold. He never found gold, but the experience gave him ideas for his short stories. The most famous of his stories is the one you are about to read, "The Luck of Roaring Camp."

The Luck of Roaring Camp

Audio starts
at line 44

There was excitement in Roaring Camp, a California mining camp in the nineteenth century. It could not be a fight. In 1850, that wasn't news.
5 Nobody paid any attention, even when French Pete and Kanaka Joe shot each other in the bar. In fact, two gamblers, playing cards, just continued their game. But now, something different was happening. Cherokee Sal, the
10 only woman in the camp, was giving birth to a child. Death was common in Roaring Camp, but a birth was a new thing.

The men sat around outside Sal's 15 cabin, wondering what to do. Finally, Kentuck, one of the leaders in the camp, said, "You go in there, Stumpy. Go in there, and see what you can do. You have experience in them things." 20 The other men agreed. Stumpy was the head of two families before he came to Roaring Camp. The men pushed Stumpy into the cabin and closed the door. 25

There were about a hundred men in Roaring Camp. All of them were either hiding from the police, or from their wives and children. But their faces and bodies showed no sign of their past lives. The worst criminal had blond hair and an angel's face. Another looked like a college professor. The bravest of the men was only five feet tall. He had a soft voice and was very shy.

As the men waited, they made bets and hoped that everything would be okay. Most of the men said Sal would pull through. Some bet the child would live. There were other bets on whether the baby would be a boy or a girl.

In the middle of their discussion, a sound came from the cabin. The men stopped to listen. It was the cry of a baby! Stumpy opened the door of the cabin. One by one, the men entered. Cherokee Sal did not pull through, but her baby boy did. He lay sleeping in a little box, and beside the box was a hat.

"Gentlemen," Stumpy said, "Please pass in at the front door, round the table, and out the back door. Them as wishes to contribute anything to the child, put it into the hat."

The contributions were all different. There was a silver box, several guns, a diamond ring, a Bible, a lady's handkerchief, a silver teaspoon, a pair of scissors, some lucky charms, and two hundred dollars in coins.

Only one thing happened as the men passed by. When Kentuck bent over to take a close look at the baby, the baby grabbed Kentuck's finger. As Kentuck took his finger away, he smiled.

■ ■ ■

In the middle of their discussion, a sound came from the cabin. The men stopped to listen. It was the cry of a baby!

■ ■ ■

The next day there was a funeral for Cherokee Sal. Then the men met to discuss what they should do with her baby. Everyone said the camp should adopt him and let Stumpy take care of him. A month later, there was another meeting to decide a name for the child. Someone said that the baby brought good luck to the camp because they were beginning to find gold. So the men suggested calling him "Luck." Stumpy didn't want him to have only one name, so he added "Tommy." The child was now Tommy Luck, but the men called him "The Luck." Stumpy became his godfather.[1]

There was a complete change in Roaring Camp. The men cleaned and painted the child's cabin. Stumpy

[1] *godfather*: a man who will take care of a child if the child's parents die

made new rules. No one was allowed to use such expressions as "Curse the luck," and loud talking wasn't allowed during The Luck's sleeping hours.

On long summer days, The Luck was carried outdoors. He lay on a blanket under the trees while the men were digging for gold. They had a great deal of luck that summer. They found more gold. Roaring Camp became rich. For the rest of the summer, the men worked to improve the camp and themselves. They washed twice a day, and they wore nice clothes. They grew flowers around their cabins.

Then winter came. Snow was deep on every hillside. The mountain creek became a river, and every river became a lake. One night rushing water broke the trees and swept over Roaring Camp. When morning came, Stumpy's cabin, near the river, was gone. A little further away, Stumpy's dead body was found. The pride, the joy, the hope of Roaring Camp disappeared.

A few men who were fortunate to still be alive saw a boat coming down the river. A man and a baby were in the boat. The men could see Kentuck lying there, badly hurt. He was holding The Luck of Roaring Camp in his arms. Sadly, they could see that the baby was not alive. "He is dead," one of them said.

Kentuck opened his eyes. "Dead," he repeated, "and I am dying too." He smiled. "Dying," he repeated. "He's a'taking me with him. Tell the boys I've got The Luck with me now." The strong man held the baby tightly. The man and baby drifted away into the river, and from the river into the sea.

1. Understanding the Story

With a partner or in a small group, discuss the following questions.

1. Why is there excitement in Roaring Camp at the beginning of the story?
2. What type of men live in Roaring Camp, and why are they there?
3. Why do the men name the baby "The Luck"?
4. How does the camp change after The Luck is born?
5. What happens when winter comes?

2. Vocabulary Comprehension

The words in the list are in the story. Find the words in the story, and try to understand their meanings. Then answer the questions that follow the list. Use your own opinions, knowledge, or experiences.

wondering	shy	adopt	creek
criminal	contribution	allow	sweep
bravest	funeral	improve	drift

1. Would it be difficult or easy for a **shy** person to make a speech?

   It would be difficult because a shy person does not want to speak in front of other people.

2. Why would you be surprised if you saw a **criminal** with the face of an angel?

   _____

3. How do you clean the floors where you live? Do you **sweep** them?

   _____

4. What color clothes do people wear at a **funeral** in your culture?

   _____

5. Should teachers **allow** students to use cell phones in their classes?

   _____

6. What is the best way to **improve** your health?

   _____

7. What is the biggest **contribution** you have made? What was it for?

_____

8. What are you **wondering** about right now?

_____

9. What is the most important thing people should think about before they **adopt** a child?

_____

10. What does it mean if a person **drifts** through life?

_____

11. Did you ever swim in a **creek**? Where was it?

_____

12. What was the **bravest** thing you ever did?

_____

3. Grammar: Count and Noncount Nouns

Common nouns are either countable or uncountable.

Count nouns can be counted (you can use *one, two, three*, etc., with count nouns). Count nouns can be singular or plural.

To make the plural of most count nouns, add *-s, -es*, or *-ies* to the singular noun.

Examples of regular plural forms:

SINGULAR	PLURAL
cabin	cabins
box	boxes
voice	voices
baby	babies
family	families

To make the plural of irregular count nouns, learn the irregular forms.

Examples of irregular plural forms:

SINGULAR	PLURAL
man	men
woman	women
child	children
wife	wives
person	people

■ *Noncount nouns* **cannot be counted in English (unless you add words such as** *a piece of, a glass of, a cup of* **+ a noncount noun).**

Examples of noncount nouns:

excitement, hair, luck, gold, snow, water

Noncount nouns are always singular. When they are used as subjects, they are followed by a singular verb.

Examples of noncount nouns as subjects:

The <u>excitement</u> was about the birth of a baby.

Good <u>luck</u> came to the camp.

River <u>water</u> rises when <u>snow</u> melts.

Be careful. Do not add *-s* to these common noncount nouns:

homework, information, equipment

■ *Practice 1*

Look at the following sentences. In the chart next to the sentences, check ✓ *count noun* or *noncount noun* for each word in **bold**. Then write the plural form of the count nouns. Use a dictionary or the grammar charts on this page and page 53 to help you.

	count noun	noncount noun	plural form
1. There was **excitement** in Roaring Camp.	___	✓	_____
2. Cherokee Sal was giving birth to a **child**.	✓	___	children
3. The men pushed Stumpy into the **cabin**.	___	___	_____
4. It was a baby's **cry**!	___	___	_____

5. He lay sleeping in a little **box**.   ____   ____   _____

6. The baby brought **luck** to the camp.   ____   ____   _____

7. The men found more **gold**.   ____   ____   _____

8. Rushing **water** broke the trees.   ____   ____   _____

9. Kentuck and the baby drifted away in
   a **boat**.   ____   ____   _____

■ *Practice 2*

Look at the following paragraphs. Underline all the common nouns. Then put
CS above all singular count nouns. Put *CP* above all plural count nouns. Put *NC*
above all noncount nouns. Use a dictionary to help you.

    In the <u>summer</u>, The Luck lay on a blanket under the trees while the men were

digging for gold. They had luck and became rich. They also worked to improve

the camp. They washed each day. They wore nice clothes. They grew flowers

around their cabins.

    Then winter came. Snow was deep on every hillside. The creek became a river.

Then it became a lake. One night, water swept over the land, and the pride, the

joy, the hope of Roaring Camp disappeared.

    A few people saw a boat with Kentuck in it. His eyes were open, but he was

dying. He told the boys he had The Luck with him. He was holding the baby in

his arms. They drifted away into the sea.

1. Sharing Ideas

With a partner or in a small group, discuss the following questions.

1. Why do you think there are no women in Roaring Camp?
2. What contributions do the men put in the hat for the child? Are any of the contributions useful for the child's life?
3. Is Stumpy a good godfather? Why or why not?
4. Which character do you think loves the child the most? Which sentences in the story tell you this?
5. Why do you think Bret Harte, the author, wrote this story?

2. Reading Between the Lines

Authors often write something that can have more than one meaning. You need to figure out what the author means. This is called *reading between the lines*. Read the following sentences from the story. Then circle the answer that shows the author's meaning. If you need help, look back at the story. Discuss your answers.

1. "You go in there, Stumpy. Go in there, and see what you can do. You have experience in them things."

   a. Stumpy was a doctor before he came to the camp.

   b. Stumpy has children of his own.

   c. Stumpy is the smartest man in the camp.

2. The worst criminal had blond hair and an angel's face. Another looked like a college professor. The bravest of the men was only five feet tall. He had a soft voice and was very shy.

   a. The men were much more dangerous than they looked.

   b. The men were all educated and kind.

   c. The men looked bad or dangerous, but they weren't really.

3. "Dying," he repeated. "He's a'taking me with him."

   a. Kentuck is badly hurt and can't leave the boat.

   b. Kentuck doesn't want the child to die alone.

   c. The child won't let go of Kentuck.

3. Analyzing the Story: Local Color

As you read on page 48, *local color* gives the reader a clear idea of the time and place of the story. Complete the chart with line numbers from the story that match the descriptions of local color in the right-hand column of the chart.

Lines	What the Lines Tell You
Lines __5__ to __7__	Drinking and violence were a normal part of everyday life at Roaring Camp.
Lines _____ to _____	The men are not very well educated and speak in an ungrammatical and casual manner.
Lines _____ to _____	Normally, the men are rough-looking and dirty and don't mind living in a dirty place.
Lines _____ to _____	The camp is in the middle of the countryside, and winters are wet and cold.

4. Summary

Put the following sentences in the correct order to summarize the story. Write the numbers 1 to 7 to show the order. The first one has been done for you.

_____ The men adopt the baby.

_____ A winter storm destroys Roaring Camp.

___1___ Cherokee Sal gives birth to a baby boy.

_____ The men name the baby "The Luck."

_____ Stumpy becomes the baby's godfather.

_____ Kentuck, holding The Luck in his arms, dies with him.

_____ The men work hard to improve Roaring Camp.

5. Writing

Do you think the story had a happy or an unhappy ending? Write your opinion.

Chapter 5
David Swan NATHANIEL HAWTHORNE

A PRE-READING

1. Think Before You Read

Answer the following questions.

1. Look at the definition of fate at the beginning of Part Two. Do you believe fate controls your future, or do you believe you control your future?
2. Have you ever been unlucky and missed a great event? Have you ever been lucky and missed something bad that could have happened to you? What happened?
3. Do you want to know what is going to happen to you tomorrow? Next year? In 20 years? Why or why not?

2. Picture Focus

With a partner, talk about the picture.

Why are people looking at the sleeping young man?

3. Key Vocabulary

Study the following key words and expressions from the story. They all relate to *sleep*. Then complete the paragraph using each word or expression once.

---

sleepy so tired that you feel you want to go to sleep

pillow a soft object you put your head on when you are resting or sleeping

fall asleep start to sleep

take a nap go to sleep for a short time, usually in the daytime

sleep soundly sleep well

awaken make someone stop sleeping

wake up stop sleeping

Some people don't _____ _____ at night even in a

comfortable bed with a nice soft _____ under their head. A small

noise can _____ them. So when they _____

_____ the next day, they are still tired. To get more sleep, these

people sometimes _____ _____ _____

during the day. And because they do that, it is even more difficult for them to

_____ _____ the next night. They just don't feel

_____.

4. Story Preview 🎧

Read the preview of the story. Then answer the question in *Making Predictions* on the next page.

> David Swan is a young man from New Hampshire. He is going to Boston to work as a clerk in his uncle's grocery store. While he is waiting for the stagecoach* that will take him to Boston, he falls asleep. While he is sleeping, three events happen. Each event could change his life forever.

* *stagecoach*: an old form of public transportation; a large, wheeled carriage pulled by horses

5. Making Predictions

From the *Story Preview*, try to predict what will happen. Circle one choice below or write your own answer. Discuss your prediction with a partner.

What will happen to David while he is sleeping?

1. David will miss the coach and lose his new job.

2. A pretty girl will stop and look at David.

3. Someone will rob David while he is sleeping.

4. _____

6. Idioms and Expressions

You will find these idioms and expressions in the story.

on foot walking

a shady spot a place that is not directly in the sun

have in mind think of a plan or idea

out of sight so you cannot be seen

make a living work for the money that pays your living expenses

I'll bet you. People say this when they are sure that something is true.

7. Literary Term: Plot

The *plot* of a story is the events that happen from the beginning of the story to the end.

Focus   As you read the story, notice all the events that happen. Notice how many of these events David, the main character, is unaware of.

About the Author

Nathaniel Hawthorne (1804–1864) was born in Salem, Massachusetts. His father was the captain of a sailing ship and died when Hawthorne was only four years old. Hawthorne went to live with his mother's large family. As a young man he read a lot. By the time he was 16, he had read almost all of Shakespeare's plays.

In 1821, Hawthorne entered Bowdoin College in Maine. There he met Henry Wadsworth Longfellow, a famous American author, and Franklin Pierce, the future president of the United States. After his graduation, Hawthorne spent the next 12 years writing. His first published book was *Twice Told Tales*, a collection of stories. "David Swan" is one of the stories. Later, Hawthorne wrote his most famous book, *The Scarlet Letter*.

When Franklin Pierce became president, he appointed Hawthorne the United States Consul at Liverpool, England. Hawthorne lived in England and Italy for many years. In 1864, he died suddenly on a trip with President Pierce.

David Swan

Audio starts
at line 26

David Swan, a young man of 20, was traveling on foot from New Hampshire to Boston. He was going to Boston to work as a clerk in his
5 uncle's grocery store. It was a very hot day, and after walking all morning in the sun, he became tired and sleepy. He found a shady spot where he could sit and wait for a stagecoach.
10 He made a pillow with the small bag of clothes he was carrying, and he put the pillow under his head. Soon David fell asleep.

While David took his nap in the shade, other people passed by him. 15 They were walking, riding horses, or sitting in carriages. Some people didn't notice David. Others laughed to see how soundly he slept. One middle-aged woman looked at him and thought he 20 looked charming in his sleep. Another rather serious-looking man thought David looked drunk. As David slept, he was completely unaware of these people and what they were thinking.

After a few minutes, a brown carriage, pulled by a pair of large horses, stopped in front of the sleeping young man. A wheel of the carriage was broken and had to be fixed. A wealthy old man and his wife stepped out of the carriage and noticed David. The woman said to her husband, "What a beautiful young man! Doesn't he look like our dead son, Henry? Shall we awaken him?"

"Why?" her husband asked, "We know nothing of his character. What do you have in mind?"

"Perhaps fate sent him to us." she replied. "Since the death of our only child, we have no one to give our money to when we die."

"Do you think he is as innocent as he looks?" her husband asked.

"Yes, let's awaken him."

But just then the driver called out, "The wheel is fixed. The carriage is ready to leave."

The old couple hurried into the carriage. They felt foolish for thinking they should awaken the stranger.

Meanwhile, David Swan enjoyed his nap.

Soon a pretty young girl walked along and stopped to fix her skirt. She blushed when she saw David asleep in the shade. Suddenly, a large bee landed on David's face. Without thinking, the young girl pushed the bee away with her handkerchief.

"How handsome he is!" the young girl thought as she looked at David sleeping.

⁶⁵ Now, this girl's father was a rich man, and he was looking for a young man like David to work for him and marry his daughter. But the girl was too shy to wake David, so she walked ⁷⁰ away. Here again, David was unaware that good fortune was close to him.

After the girl was out of sight, two evil-looking men came to the spot where David slept. These men made ⁷⁵ their living by stealing from other people. Finding David asleep, one man said to the other, "Do you see that bag under his head?"

The second man nodded.

⁸⁰ The first man said, "I'll bet you he has money in that bag. Let's take it."

"But what if he wakes up?" the second man asked.

The first man opened his coat and ⁸⁵ showed his friend a large knife.

The two men approached the sleeping David. One man held his knife near David while the other man looked in David's bag.

⁹⁰ At that moment, a dog came between the two men.

"We can't do anything now. The dog's master must be near." The two men ran from the spot while David continued to sleep. This time, David ⁹⁵ was unaware that death was close to him.

■ ■ ■

After the girl was out of sight, two evil-looking men came to the spot where David slept.

■ ■ ■

A few minutes later, a stagecoach came. David quickly woke up when he heard the noisy wheels of the coach. ¹⁰⁰

"Hello, driver," David shouted, "Will you take another passenger?"

"Sure!" answered the driver.

David climbed up to the seat next to the driver, and the stagecoach ¹⁰⁵ continued along the road to Boston.

That afternoon, while David slept, he was unaware of three events that could have changed his destiny. In that one hour, David Swan never ¹¹⁰ knew that fate almost brought him wealth, love, and death.

1. Understanding the Story

With a partner or in a small group, discuss the following questions.

1. Why is David traveling from New Hampshire to Boston?
2. What does the middle-aged woman think of David? How is her opinion different from the opinion of the serious-looking man?
3. What does the wealthy old woman want to give David?
4. What could the pretty young girl's father give David?
5. What do the evil-looking men want from David?

2. Vocabulary Comprehension

The words in the list are in the story. Read the sentences below from the story. Then circle the letter of the best meaning of the **bold** word in each sentence.

carriages	unaware	foolish	nodded
charming	character	handsome	approached
drunk	innocent	evil	passenger

1. They were walking, riding horses, or sitting in **carriages**.
   a. cars
   b. coaches pulled by horses
   c. park benches

2. One middle-aged woman looked at him and thought he looked **charming** in his sleep.
   a. like a nice man
   b. like a poor man
   c. like a baby

3. Another rather serious-looking man thought David looked **drunk**.
   a. very dark and dangerous
   b. like he had too much alcohol
   c. sick

4. As David slept, he was completely **unaware** of these people and what they were thinking.
   a. not knowing
   b. not interested
   c. not showing

5. "Do you think he is as **innocent** as he looks?" her husband asked.
   a. young
   b. healthy
   c. good and kind

6. "Why?" her husband asked, "We know nothing of his **character**."
   a. life
   b. education
   c. qualities

7. The old couple hurried into the carriage. They felt **foolish** for thinking they should awaken the stranger.
   a. happy
   b. unwise
   c. sad

8. "How **handsome** he is!" the young girl thought as she looked at David sleeping.
   a. rich
   b. attractive
   c. unintelligent

9. After the girl was out of sight, two **evil**-looking men came to the spot where David slept.
   a. angry
   b. strange
   c. bad

10. The second man **nodded**.
    a. moved his head to agree
    b. moved his head to disagree
    c. said nothing

11. The two men **approached** the sleeping David.
    a. came close to
    b. hit
    c. looked carefully at

12. "Hello, driver," David shouted. "Will you take another **passenger**?"
    a. bag
    b. direction
    c. person

3. Grammar: Articles

A, *an*, and *the* are called *articles*. Articles come before nouns. There are many rules for using articles. The following are some basic ones.

Articles with singular count nouns

Use *a* or *an* with singular count nouns when you are giving new or general information to your listener or reader. Use *the* with singular count nouns when you are giving the information for the second time or when the information is specific.

Be careful. Use *an* instead of *a* before a vowel sound.

Examples:
David made a pillow. He put the pillow under his head.
He slept for an hour. Many things happened to David during the hour.
(*Hour* does not begin with a vowel letter, but it begins with a vowel sound.)

Articles with plural count nouns

Do not use any article for plural count nouns when you are giving new or general information to your listener or reader. Use *the* for plural count nouns when you are giving information for the second time or when the information is specific.

Examples:
They were riding horses or sitting in carriages.
The horses were large, and the carriages were beautiful.

Articles with noncount nouns

Do not use *a* or *an* for noncount nouns.

Do not use any article when the noncount noun is giving general information.

Use *the* for noncount nouns when they are specific.

Examples:
I like money.
Thank you for the money you lent me.

■ *Practice 1*

In the following sentences, fill in the blank lines with *a*, *an*, or *the*. If no article is necessary, leave the line blank.

1. __A__ carriage stopped in front of David. A wealthy old couple was sitting in

   __the__ carriage.

2. _____ girl saw David sleeping. _____ girl thought that David was handsome.

3. The girl saw _____ bee on David's face. She pushed _____ bee away.

4. _____ evil-looking man saw David sleeping. _____ man wanted to take

   David's bag.

5. Soon _____ dog came. The men ran away when they saw _____ dog.

6. A stagecoach, filled with _____ passengers, came. _____ passengers were on

   their way to Boston.

7. David looked for _____ seat. He took _____ seat next to the driver.

■ *Practice 2*

Circle the correct noun phrase for each sentence.

1. David, (*a young man of 20*)/ *young man of 20* / *a young men of 20*, was traveling

   to Boston.

2. The carriage was pulled by a pair of *the horses* / *horses* / *horse*.

3. *A middle-aged widow* / *An middle-aged widow* / *Middle-aged widow* looked

   at David.

4. A wealthy old man and his wife looked at David. *Old woman* / *An old woman* /

   The old woman said to her husband, "What a beautiful young man!"

5. A girl pushed a bee away from David's face with *handkerchief* / *handkerchiefs* /

   a handkerchief.

6. Two men tried to steal *a bags* / *a bag* / *bag* from David.

7. David lost his chance for *a wealth and happiness* / *wealth and happiness* /

   the wealth and happiness.

1. Sharing Ideas

With a partner or in a small group, discuss the following questions.

1. What do you think might happen if the pretty young girl awakens David?
2. Why does the wealthy old woman think fate sent David to her and her husband?
3. Do you think David is more a lucky man or an unlucky man? Explain your answer.
4. Do you think David will work hard in his uncle's store when he gets to Boston? Why or why not?
5. What does the story tell us about fate?

2. Reading Between the Lines

Authors often write something that can have more than one meaning. You need to figure out what the author means. This is called *reading between the lines*. Read the following sentences from the story. Then circle the answer that shows the author's meaning. If you need help, look back at the story. Discuss your answers.

1. The old couple hurried into the carriage. They felt foolish for thinking they should awaken the stranger.

    a. The couple was sorry that they missed their chance to meet David.

    b. The couple realized it was a bad idea to awaken David.

    c. The couple was afraid of David and wanted to get away quickly.

2. She blushed when she saw David asleep in the shade.

    a. The girl thought that David was very attractive and that she might fall in love with him.

    b. The girl was thinking that her father would be pleased that she found a possible husband.

    c. The girl's face got red because she was feeling hot on such a hot and sunny day.

3. "But what if he wakes up?" the second man asked. The first man opened his coat and showed his friend a large knife.

    a. The first man was going to kill David if he woke up.

    b. The first man wanted to kill his friend.

    c. The first man wanted his friend to see how brave he was.

3. Analyzing the Story: Plot

As you read on page 60, the *plot* is the events that happen in a story. A good way to remember the plot is to make a timeline and show the events in the order they happened. The plot of "David Swan" has several events that happen while David is sleeping. Put the events in the timeline. Use your own words. Work with a partner.

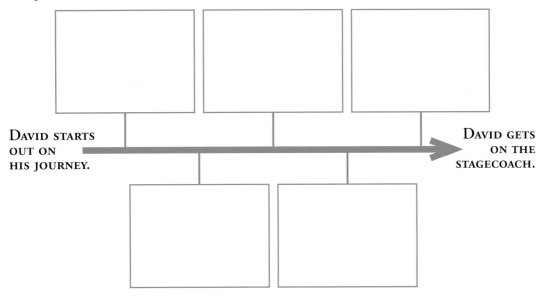

4. Summary

Put the following sentences in the correct order to summarize the story. Write the numbers 1 to 7 to show the order. The first one has been done for you.

_____ A pretty girl pushes away a bee that is on David's face.

_____ A dog saves David from being killed.

_____ While waiting for the stagecoach, David falls asleep.

_____ Two evil men try to take David's bag.

_____ An elderly couple almost decide to awaken David and adopt him.

_____ A middle-aged woman stares at David and admires his face.

___1___ David Swan is on his way to Boston to work in his uncle's store.

5. Writing

Describe what you think David's life is like when he lives in Boston.

Chapter 6

The Pace of Youth STEPHEN CRANE

1. Think Before You Read

Answer the following questions.

1. How do you know when you are in love with someone? What happens to you?
2. Did you ever have a boyfriend or girlfriend your parents didn't like? What did your parents say or do when they didn't like the boyfriend or girlfriend?
3. Should parents let their children love anyone the children want? Why or why not?

2. Picture Focus

With a partner, talk about the picture.

Who is the man looking out the window? Why does he look angry?

3. Key Vocabulary

Study the following key words and expressions from the story. They all relate to *people having feelings for each other*. Then complete the paragraph using each word or expression once.

---

make eyes at stare at someone and try to get his or her attention because you like that person

smile when the corners of your mouth are turned up to show you are happy

fall in love begin to love another person

hold hands have one hand holding another person's hand

passion strong, deep feeling of love, hatred, or anger

When two people _____ _____

_____, they show their feelings for each other in different ways. At

a party, they might _____ _____

_____ each other and not pay attention to other people around

them. You can see a _____ on their faces as they talk with each

other. They usually _____ _____ as they walk

together. Because they are young, they think their _____ will

last forever.

4. Story Preview 🎧

Read the preview of the story. Then answer the question in *Making Predictions* on the next page.

This is a story about two young people, Frank and Lizzie, who fall in love. They both work for the young woman's father, Stimson, who owns a merry-go-round. The young man and woman often smile and stare at each other while they are working. The father does not like their relationship and warns them to stop looking at each other.

5. Making Predictions

From the *Story Preview*, try to predict what will happen. Circle one choice below or write your own answer. Discuss your prediction with a partner.

What will happen to the young couple?

1. The young man will find a new girlfriend.

2. The young woman will obey her father and stop paying attention to the young man.

3. The young couple will get married.

4. _____

6. Idioms and Expressions

You will find these idioms and expressions in the story.

---

show off do something to attract attention to yourself

business as usual everything is normal

come to the rescue help someone who is in trouble

catch up reach someone or something that is ahead of you

run away together leave family and friends far away so that you can live together or get married

take off leave quickly

---

7. Literary Term: Theme

A story's *theme* is the author's main idea or purpose in writing the story. It is what the author wants us to think about when we have finished reading. A good author doesn't tell readers directly what the theme of the story is. Readers have to find the theme as they read. The characters, setting, and plot create the theme. Sometimes a story has several themes.

Focus As you read the story, think about the theme and what opinion the author is trying to share with you.

About the Author

Stephen Crane (1871–1900) is most famous for his novel *The Red Badge of Courage*, which was published in 1895. *The Red Badge of Courage* is the story of a soldier in the American Civil War. It is one of the first modern novels about war.

Crane, the son of a Methodist minister, was born in Newark, New Jersey. He briefly attended college and then moved to New York City to become a writer and journalist.

Crane spent his last two years living in England and died in Germany at age 28. Some of his other famous works are *The Open Boat* and *Maggie: A Girl of the Streets*. "The Pace of Youth" takes place in the 1890s and is one of Crane's lighter stories. It deals with love and youth instead of war and death.

The Pace of Youth

Audio starts at line 54

Stimson stood in the corner of his office staring at the young man. "He must stop making eyes at Lizzie. If he doesn't stop, I'll take away his job."

5   Then Stimson looked up at the sign, "Stimson's Mammoth Merry-Go-Round." The sign was huge. Each letter was six feet tall. It glowed with light and could be seen from three
10 blocks away. He stood proudly looking at the sign. He heard the sound of the ocean mixed with the voices of people on the beach. As he looked to the north, he saw the horizon where the
15 sky met the sea. He saw a sailboat far out in the water and a bird drifting slowly in the air.

Stimson then looked back at his merry-go-round. There was a circle of animals – lions, giraffes, camels, and 20 horses. They were painted in bright colors and shined in the mirrors in the center of the merry-go-round. Their wooden legs moved up and down in an endless race while the 25 music played.

Stimson could hear children laughing as they sat on the colorful animals and pretended to be in a real race. Some parents rode with the 30 very young children who couldn't ride alone. A young man stood on top of the narrow wooden platform making sure the children did not get hurt on 35 the merry-go-round.

This young man was the one Stimson was angry at. His name was Frank, and he and Lizzie looked at each other many times during the day. 40 Lizzie worked in a ticket booth near the merry-go-round. Frank looked at Lizzie, and Lizzie looked at Frank.

Sometimes Lizzie saw Frank staring at her. She would then turn her 45 head quickly to show that she wasn't interested in him. At other times, she worried about him falling off the narrow wooden platform. Frank showed off by standing very close to 50 its edge. The relationship between these two young people continued in silence. They communicated with smiles and stares.

One day, Stimson walked over to 55 Frank and said, "This must stop."

Frank couldn't understand how Stimson knew about his love for Lizzie. Stimson continued, "I see you making eyes at my daughter, and I 60 see her smiling at you. If you want to keep your job, stop this nonsense."

Frank was quiet as Stimson turned around and walked to the ticket booth. Stimson approached Lizzie and 65 said, "Stop smiling at that fool. I told him, and I'm telling you. Stop staring and smiling. You have work to do."

Lizzie was very quiet, too. She didn't look at her father and just played with the money on the shelf 70 in the ticket booth. Stimson walked away smiling. He was proud of his behavior.

"That's the end of that. There'll be no more nonsense around here. It will 75 be business as usual."

Then he stood outside smoking a cigar and watching his merry-go-round.

One evening, a week later, Lizzie's 80 friend Jennie came over to the ticket booth and asked Lizzie if she wanted to walk along the beach after work. Frank saw them talking and followed them. At first, Frank was 85 afraid to approach the girls because he remembered Stimson's warning. He was a coward, but then he found the courage to get closer. In a weak voice he called out, "Lizzie." 90

Lizzie turned suddenly and said, "Frank, you scared me."

"I'm sorry," Frank said.

Then Jennie came to the rescue. "Come and walk on the beach with 95 us, Frank."

Frank smiled and joined them. After a while, Jennie said, "I'd like to sit here and look at the sea. You two go on. I'll catch up with you later." 100

They asked her to join them, but she said no. Finally, the young couple walked on without her.

"Jennie's really nice," said Lizzie.

"Yes, she is," Frank agreed. 105

They walked silently. Then Lizzie said, "You were angry at me last week."

"No, I wasn't."

"Yes, you were. You didn't look at me once."

"No, I wasn't angry. I was just pretending."

"Oh, were you?" Lizzie said laughing.

Frank looked at Lizzie and knew he was falling in love with her. They held hands and walked back along the beach. When they came back to where Jennie was sitting, she could see the love in their eyes and in their smiles.

A few weeks later, Stimson had to go to the city. When he returned, he found the man who sold popcorn sitting in the ticket booth. Nobody was standing on the wooden platform.

"Where is Lizzie?" he asked the popcorn man.

"They went to your house."

Stimson ran to his house and found his wife crying.

"Where's Lizzie?" he yelled.

"Oh, John. They ran away together. They drove by in the horse and carriage a few minutes ago so Lizzie could say goodbye. Before I could ask where they were going, they took off."

"Get my rifle.[1] Do you hear? Get my rifle."

Stimson always told his wife what to do, and she always obeyed. But this time she said, "No, John, not the rifle."

[1] *rifle*: a long gun

Stimson ran down the street looking for a horse and carriage. He found one and jumped in the back. He told the driver to follow Frank and Lizzie's carriage. The driver pushed the horse as hard as he could, and Stimson stood up like a general riding into battle.

"Hurry, hurry. Make your horse go faster, faster."

The carriage ahead of them went faster, and soon the distance between them grew larger and larger. The young couple with the energy of youth flew ahead. They had the power of dreams. They flew with the pace of youth. They would fly into the future with hope and passion.

At last, the driver said to Stimson, "It's no good. We can't catch them."

Stimson knew he had lost. He was just a powerless old man. He was hot and tired and his head felt cool. He touched his head and realized he forgot his hat.

AFTER READING

1. *Understanding the Story*

With a partner or in a small group, discuss the following questions.

1. How do Frank and Lizzie communicate with each other while they are working?
2. What kind of man is Mr. Stimson? Describe him.
3. How do Frank and Lizzie behave around Mr. Stimson?
4. How does Mrs. Stimson behave around her husband?
5. How does Jennie help Frank and Lizzie?

2. *Vocabulary Comprehension*

■ *Practice 1*

The words on the left are in the story. Match each word to the correct definition on the right. Write the letter of the definition on the blank line.

___e___	1. pretend	a. the way a person does or says things
_____	2. narrow	b. really mad at someone or about something
_____	3. communicate	c. how fast or slow someone walks or runs
_____	4. nonsense	d. the ability to be active without becoming tired
_____	5. behavior	e. act as if something is true when it is not
_____	6. warning	f. the length of space between two places
_____	7. coward	g. ability to do dangerous or difficult things
_____	8. courage	h. not wide; a small distance from one side to the other
_____	9. couple	i. do what someone tells you to do
_____	10. angry	j. someone who is not brave
_____	11. obey	k. two people or things together
_____	12. distance	l. talk or write to someone; send a message through one's behavior
_____	13. energy	m. foolish words or actions
_____	14. pace	n. something that tells or shows you that something bad will happen

Find the words from *Practice 1* in the word search box. The words are written across or down.

```
A N G R Y Z C O U R A G E L Q E P I O E U
S A R N O N S E N S E P G J W A R N I N G
D R A C O M M U N I C A T E K Q E B M E F
K R W G B D I S T A N C E H R B T A W R J
I O M B E H A V I O R E I A D T E Q C G V
E W Q S Y Z R C O W A R D X W O N P I Y B
C O U P L E A W L Q F V S P Y X D N R E X
```

3. Grammar: Pronouns

Pronouns are words that can replace nouns. There are different types of pronouns. Two basic types are *subject* pronouns and *object* pronouns.

■ Subject pronouns are *I, you, he, she, it, we,* and *they*. They are used as the subjects of verbs.

Example:

Stimson was angry. He did not want Frank and Lizzie looking at each other.

■ Object pronouns are *me, you, him, her, it, us,* and *them*. They are used as the objects of verbs or of prepositions.

Examples:

Jennie and Lizzie walked down the beach. Frank followed them.
(object of the verb *followed*)

Frank and Lizzie were in love. Jennie could see the love between them.
(object of the preposition *between*)

When you use a pronoun, it must be the same gender (masculine or feminine) or number (singular or plural) as the noun it replaces.

Examples:
Frank = he / him
Lizzie = she / her
Frank and Lizzie = they / them
the merry-go-round = it

■ *Practice 1*

The following paragraph has eight subject pronouns and nine object pronouns. Circle the subject pronouns and underline the object pronouns.

Frank and Lizzie worked for Stimson's Mammoth Merry-Go-Round. During the day, (they) made eyes at each other. Sometimes Lizzie saw Frank staring at her. She would pretend she wasn't interested in him. Frank didn't know that Lizzie was in love with him, but Frank was in love with her. Stimson did not want Frank and Lizzie to look at each other. He told them to stop it. Later they ran away. Stimson's wife told him that they left in a carriage. Stimson could see it in the distance, and he realized he could not catch up with them.

■ *Practice 2*

The following sentences are from the story. Circle the subject or object pronouns in ***b***, and underline the noun or nouns in ***a*** that the pronouns replace.

1. a. Stimson stood in the corner of his office staring at the young man.

   b. "(He) must stop making eyes at Lizzie."

2. a. The sign was huge. Each letter was six feet tall.

   b. It glowed with light and could be seen from three blocks away.

3. a. There was a circle of animals – lions, giraffes, camels, and horses.

   b. They were painted in bright colors and shined in the mirrors in the center of the merry-go-round.

4. a. The relationship between these two young people continued in silence.

   b. They communicated with smiles and stares.

5. a. . . . Lizzie's friend Jennie came over to the ticket booth and asked Lizzie if she wanted to walk along the beach after work.

   b. Frank saw them talking . . . .

6. a. At first Frank was afraid to approach the girls because he remembered Stimson's warning.

   b. He was a coward, but then he found the courage to get closer.

7. a. "Jennie's really nice," said Lizzie.

   b. "Yes, she is," Frank agreed.

8. a. Frank looked at Lizzie and knew he was falling in love with her.

   b. They held hands and walked back along the beach.

9. a. Stimson always told his wife what to do . . .

   b. . . . and she always obeyed.

10. a. The young couple with the energy of youth flew ahead.

    b. They had the power of dreams.

D THINKING ABOUT THE STORY

1. Sharing Ideas

With a partner or in a small group, discuss the following questions.

1. Why do you think Mr. Stimson does not like Frank and Lizzie's relationship?
2. Do you like Mr. Stimson? Why or why not?
3. Why does Jennie decide not to continue on the walk with Frank and Lizzie?
4. How do you think Mr. Stimson feels at the end of the story?
5. Are you glad that Mr. Stimson could not catch up with Frank and Lizzie? Why or why not?

2. Reading Between the Lines

Authors often write something that can have more than one meaning. You need to figure out what the author means. This is called *reading between the lines*. Read the following sentences from the story. Then circle the answer that shows the author's meaning. If you need help, look back at the story. Discuss your answers.

1. She didn't look at her father and just played with the money on the shelf in the ticket booth.
   a. Lizzie was afraid of her father.
   b. Lizzie was busy selling tickets.
   c. Lizzie was happy and was thinking of Frank.

2. After a while, Jennie said, "I'd like to sit here and look at the sea. You two go on. I'll catch up with you later."
   a. Jennie is very tired and wants to rest.
   b. Jennie wants Lizzie and Frank to be alone together.
   c. Jennie is sad that Frank likes Lizzie.

3. Stimson always told his wife what to do, and she always obeyed. But this time she said, "No, John, not the rifle."
   a. Stimson's wife is afraid her husband will kill the young couple.
   b. Stimson's wife doesn't want to obey her husband anymore.
   c. Stimson's wife wants her husband to hurt the couple, but not kill them.

4. He was just a powerless old man.

    a. Stimson did not have the energy and passion of youth.

    b. Stimson suddenly became old.

    c. Stimson lost his power over other people.

3. Analyzing the Story: Theme

As you read on page 72, the *theme* of a story gives the author's opinion about life. But remember, the author doesn't tell you the theme; you must find it from the words in the story.

One theme for "The Pace of Youth" is "Love is powerful." One example from the story that matches this theme is in the chart below. Find two more examples in the story that match this theme and put them in the chart.

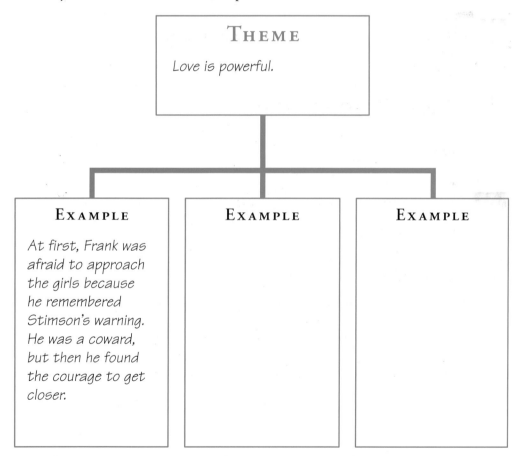

THEME

Love is powerful.

EXAMPLE

At first, Frank was afraid to approach the girls because he remembered Stimson's warning. He was a coward, but then he found the courage to get closer.

EXAMPLE

EXAMPLE

A story may have more than one theme. Find another theme from the story and make a chart like the one above. Share your charts with a partner.

4. Summary

Put the following sentences in the correct order to summarize the story. Write the numbers 1 to 6 to show the order. The first one has been done for you.

_____ Stimson tells Frank he'll fire him if he doesn't stop looking at his daughter.

___1___ Stimson sees Frank and Lizzie staring and smiling at each other.

_____ Frank and Lizzie walk on the beach and realize they're in love.

_____ When Stimson goes to his house, he finds his wife crying.

_____ Stimson chases the couple, but they get away.

_____ Stimson finds out that Frank and Lizzie ran away.

5. Writing

What do you think Mr. and Mrs. Stimson say to each other when Mr. Stimson comes back home after Frank and Lizzie run away? Continue writing their conversation below. Use some of the new words and expressions you learned in this chapter.

Mrs. Stimson: Did you see them, John?

Mr. Stimson: Yes, but I couldn't catch up with them.

Mrs. Stimson: _____

Mr. Stimson: _____

Mrs. Stimson: _____

Mr. Stimson: _____

Mrs. Stimson: _____

Mr. Stimson: _____

Summing Up

A | TAKE A CLOSER LOOK

1. Theme Comparison: The Role of Fate

Some people believe that although we make plans for the future, fate actually controls our lives and what happens in them. All three stories in Part Two deal with *the role of fate*. All of the characters have experiences that control their futures, and as each story ends, we understand the fate of the characters.

With a partner, discuss the following questions.

1. What forces change the fate of The Luck, Kentuck, Stumpy, David Swan, Lizzie, Frank, and Mr. Stimson?
2. How would the stories end if fate did not enter the lives of the characters?
3. How do the characters act after fate changes their plans?

2. Freewriting

Write the word *fate* on the top of a sheet of paper. Then write any words that come into your mind when you think of *fate*. For 15 minutes, write about your own life. Do you remember a time or situation that was changed by fate? How did your life change? What did you think about at the time? How do you feel about it now?

B | REVIEW

1. Grammar Review

Rewrite the following paragraph on a sheet of paper. Change the underlined words to the correct *count nouns*, *noncount nouns*, *articles*, and *pronouns*.

In <u>a</u> first story of Part Two, <u>the</u> baby comes to Roaring Camp. All the <u>mans</u> of <u>a</u> camp love <u>a</u> baby. <u>Him</u> brings good <u>lucks</u> to the camp, and the <u>mans</u> find <u>golds</u>. In the end, a terrible storm makes the <u>babies</u> and <u>the</u> Kentuck drift away down the river. In the second <u>stories</u>, David Swan falls asleep under <u>the</u> tree. A young girl stops by and looks at <u>he</u>. <u>A</u> girl is very pretty. She thinks <u>a</u> sleeping young man is handsome. <u>The</u> David wakes up and never knows <u>a</u> events that happened to <u>her</u>. In <u>a</u> final story, two young <u>lover</u> run away together. <u>A</u> father of the girl is very angry, but <u>she</u> is old and tired and knows he must let <u>they</u> go.

2. Vocabulary Review

The definitions under *Across* and *Down* are for vocabulary words in Part Two. Read the definitions and complete the crossword puzzle with the correct vocabulary words.

Across

1. Something that tells or shows you that something bad will happen
3. The belief that something good will happen
7. Attractive; good-looking (usually a male)
10. Legally become the parent of someone else's child
12. Bad; harmful
13. Ability to do dangerous or difficult things
15. A soft object you put your head on when you are resting or sleeping

Down

2. Get better or make something better
4. Nice; pleasant
5. The way a person does or says things
6. When the corners of your mouth are turned up to show you are happy
8. The length of space between two places
9. Tell people what you think will happen in the future, and usually ask for money if you are right
11. So tired that you feel you want to go to sleep
14. Let someone do something; give someone permission

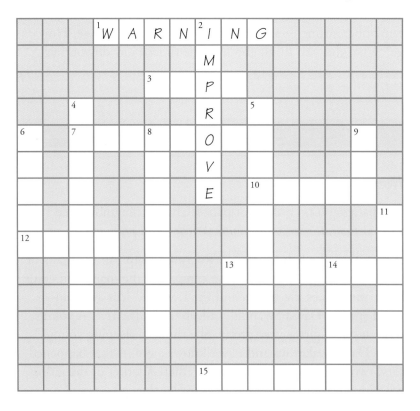

Filling Out the Elements Chart

This chart shows the five basic elements of a short story. You can find definitions for these elements on page 170. Some of these elements have been filled out for "The Luck of Roaring Camp." Complete the chart. Then copy the blank chart on page xvii and fill it out for "David Swan" or "The Pace of Youth" or for both stories. Share your charts with a partner or in a small group.

Elements of _____ The Luck of Roaring Camp _____
(name of story)

SETTING

CHARACTERS

PLOT
The only woman in the miners' camp dies while giving birth to a baby boy. The miners adopt the child. They love him and take good care of him. In the winter, a big storm comes, and many men lose their lives. The baby dies in the arms of one of the men who loves him.

CONFLICT
The conflict is between the men and the forces of nature.

THEME(S)
The birth of a child can change people's lives.
Nature wins over all.

Mystery and Fantasy

MOST OF US like to read about strange events, and sometimes we even like to be scared. That is why mystery and fantasy are so popular in literature. As readers, we try to understand the truth of a story – what is real and what is fiction. As we read these stories, we love to try to figure out what is really happening in the story and why it is happening. We also try to figure out what will happen to the characters.

■ As you read the stories in Part Three, try to solve the mysteries in them. When will the wife of a lonely Californian man return home after visiting her family? Who is the strange guest who comes to a masquerade party? What really happens to the school teacher in Sleepy Hollow?

 Chapter 9

THE LEGEND OF
SLEEPY HOLLOW
– Washington Irving

Chapter 7
The Californian's Tale MARK TWAIN

A PRE-READING

1. Think Before You Read

Answer the following questions.

1. In "The Luck of Roaring Camp" (Chapter 4), you learned about the Gold Rush and the mining camps in California in the 1800s. How did the men, or miners, live at that time?
2. Did the men live with their families? Do you think these men were lonely? Why or why not?
3. What do you think homes were like in the small towns and mining camps of California in the 1800s?

2. Picture Focus

With a partner, talk about the picture.

Where are the two men? What are they talking about?

3. Key Vocabulary

Study the following key words and expressions from the story. They all relate to *a home and its contents*. Then complete the paragraph using each word or expression once.

> **log cabins** small houses built with logs from trees
>
> **cottages** small houses
>
> **decorated** added things to a place to make it look nice
>
> **a woman's touch** the style a woman puts in a house
>
> **cozy** warm and comfortable
>
> **washstand** a wooden piece of furniture used as a sink
>
> **towel** a cloth used to dry something that is wet

During the Gold Rush days, men lived in simple _____

_____ near rivers and streams. Later, as the men got married and

started families, they often built small houses closer to town. These small houses

were called _____. They often had flowers and gardens, and the

women _____ them nicely. However, these small houses did not

have running water inside. Instead, people usually had a wooden

_____ with a bowl on top, and they put this in their bedrooms.

People washed their hands and face in the bowl. A _____ hung on

a bar nearby. These small houses could be very _____, especially

with _____ _____ _____.

4. Story Preview 🎧

Read the preview of the story. Then answer the question in *Making Predictions* on
the next page.

> A young man meets an older man named Henry. Henry lives in a lovely
> cottage. Henry has a young wife who is away visiting her family. The young
> man sees a photo of the wife and wants to meet her. He agrees to stay with
> Henry for a few days to meet Henry's wife when she returns home.

5. Making Predictions

From the *Story Preview*, try to predict what will happen. Circle one choice below or write your own answer. Discuss your prediction with a partner.

What will happen when Henry's wife returns?

1. The young man will fall in love with her.

2. Henry's wife will tell the young man where to find gold.

3. Henry's wife will not return home.

4. _____

6. Idioms and Expressions

You will find these idioms and expressions in the story.

> **dropped by** visited
>
> **sent regards** sent good wishes; said "hello"
>
> **check your watch** look at the time on your watch
>
> **felt sorry for someone** felt sad for someone else's unhappiness
>
> **take turns** do something one person at a time
>
> **keep someone company** stay with someone, especially someone who is lonely

7. Literary Term: Surprise Ending

Some stories have a *surprise ending*. The ending can be sudden and unexpected. When you read the story, you expect it to end one way, but the writer surprises you with a different ending. Then if you read the story again, you can often find sentences that give you a clue* about the ending.

Focus   As you read the story, think of how you expect the story to end. Are you surprised at the end? After you read the story, read it again. Notice which sentences in the story give you a clue about the ending.

* *clue*: information that helps you find an answer, solve a problem, or understand something

About the Author

Mark Twain (1835–1910) was born Samuel Clemens in Florida, Missouri. Mark Twain is the name Samuel Clemens used when he wrote stories. Twain is one of America's best-loved writers. His sense of humor and imagination helped make him famous as a writer and a speaker. He traveled all over the United States and the world talking to people.

Twain often wrote about life in the South in the 1800s. He used realistic characters and dialogue to tell his stories about intolerance[1] and friendship. Two of his most famous novels are *The Adventures of Tom Sawyer* and *The Adventures of Huckleberry Finn*. These books have been translated into many languages.

The Californian's Tale

Audio starts at line 76

I was mining in California, and I hoped to find gold. The weeks and months passed, and I never found my fortune.

5 It was beautiful out there, but very lonely. I used to live in a city, but now I saw only fields and trees and once in a while, an old log cabin. When the easy gold was gone, 10 almost everyone left. I was alone for a long time. And although I liked the peace and quiet, I was happy to see another human. He was a man about forty-five years old. He was standing 15 next to a rose-covered cottage. The front yard was filled with flowers. His name was Henry, and he invited me into his cottage.

I thanked him and was happy to see his lovely home. The cottage was 20 decorated with a woman's touch. There were pictures hanging on the walls and rugs on the floors. There were books, vases, and other pretty decorations. His cottage was very 25 cozy. After living in a tent for many months, this was a wonderful change. He saw me smiling as I sat in a wooden chair.

"It's all her work," he said with a 30

1 *intolerance*: not accepting other people's race, religion, customs, or ideas

loving voice. I watched him smooth a scarf which lay over the arm of a chair. It was like the pats a mother gives a child after she combs and brushes the child's hair. "She always does that. I see her fix all these things so often that I can do it the way she does."

He took me into the bedroom so I could wash my hands. In the corner there was a washstand. I looked around the room, and once again I saw all the touches of a woman's taste. The towels were clean and white, and the soap sat in a floral soap dish. He kept smiling at me as I washed my hands and dried them with a towel.

Henry looked at me, and then he looked at a small photo sitting on a shelf. It was the photo of a beautiful, young woman.

"Is that your wife?" I asked.

"Yes, she was nineteen on her last birthday."

"Where is she now? When will she return?"

"Oh, she's away. She went to visit her family. They live about fifty miles away. She left two weeks ago."

"When do you expect her back?"

"This is Wednesday. She'll be back on Saturday at about nine o'clock at night."

"I'm sorry, I won't meet her because I have to leave before Saturday."

"Leave? Oh, she'll be so disappointed."

I looked at her photograph. I felt a deep, strong need to meet her.

"You see, she likes to have people come and stay with us. She likes to meet people who know things and can talk. She knows a lot and reads books. She'll be so disappointed. Please stay. It's only a few days from now. Please stay until Saturday."

Henry picked up the photograph and handed it to me.

"There now, tell her to her face that you can't stay to meet her."

When I looked at her face a second time, I knew I would stay. "Okay, my friend. I'll stay and meet your lovely wife."

We talked that night mostly about her. The next day was Thursday, and in the evening, an old miner dropped by for a visit. "I came by to ask about your wife, Henry. When is she coming home? Did you hear from her?"

"Oh yes, I received a letter. Would you like to hear it, Tom?"

"Sure, Henry."

Henry took the letter out of his wallet and read it to us. At the end of the letter, she sent regards to Tom, Joe, and Charley, and some other neighbors. As Henry finished reading the letter, he said, "Tom, you are doing it again. Take your hands away from your eyes. You always do that when I read a letter from her. I'll tell her when she comes back."

"Oh no, Henry, I'm getting old, you know, and any disappointment makes me cry. I thought she'd be here herself, and now there's just a letter."

"Tom, everyone knows she's coming back on Saturday."

"Yes, Henry. I guess I did know that, but I forgot. I'll be sure to come back on Saturday." Tom said goodnight to us and left.

On Friday another old man came to visit from his cabin about a mile away. His name was Joe, and he said he and some of the other neighbors would come on Saturday to celebrate her return. Once again, Henry read her letter, and once again I saw tears in another old man's eyes.

Finally, on Saturday I kept looking at my watch while waiting for her to arrive. Henry noticed and said, "You're not worried about her are you?"

"No," I answered. "I always check my watch when I expect someone."

Four times Henry walked up the road and looked for her. "I'm worried," he said. "I know she's not due until nine o'clock, but maybe something happened. You don't think anything happened, do you?"

I hardly knew the man, but I felt sorry for him. He seemed like a child. I was glad when another friend, Charley, arrived at the house. He began talking to Henry. "Now you know nothing has happened. Why don't you go inside and take a nap so you'll be wide awake when she arrives?" Henry went into the bedroom.

It was then that I said to Charley, "Please stay here with me. She doesn't know me. We've never met, and I only stayed because it seemed so important to Henry. If Henry's sleeping, I don't want her to be uncomfortable to see a stranger."

"You won't be meeting her, young man. She's been missing for nineteen years. Yes, she was only nineteen when she went to visit her family. She never arrived home that night. The horse came home without her. We searched the woods for weeks, but there was no sign of her.

"Henry's never been the same. He does all right during the year, but as the anniversary of her disappearance approaches, we all take turns being with him. On the actual day, Tom, Joe, and I always come to be with him. We decorate the house with flowers and help Henry get through the day. There used to be a lot more of us in the early years, but we're getting old. Now there are just the three of us. Joe and Tom will be here soon. We'll sing some songs and keep him company until he falls asleep. We stay with him all night. Tomorrow he'll be okay and just remember his beautiful young wife. She sure was a lovely young woman. We all miss her."

93
The Californian's Tale

C | AFTER READING

1. Understanding the Story

With a partner or in a small group, discuss the following questions.

1. How does the young man meet Henry?
2. In what ways does Henry's house show "a woman's touch"?
3. How do Henry's friends behave when they visit him?
4. What does the young man learn about Henry's wife at the end of the story?

2. Vocabulary Comprehension

The words in the list are in the story. Find the words in the story. They are not listed in order. Try to understand their meanings. Then read the paragraph below. Replace the words in parentheses with words from the box. Use each word once.

human	anniversary	disappointed	invites
tears	expects	celebrate	disappearance
tent	taste	floral	scarf

The narrator of the story, a young man, lives alone in a (moveable house that is made of cloth) _____*tent*_____ outside the city. He never sees another (person) _____, but one day he meets Henry. Henry lives in a cozy cottage, and he (asks) _____ the young man to visit him. The cottage has flowers outside and (flowered) _____ dishes inside. The decorations show good (ability to enjoy and use beautiful things) _____. He watches Henry smooth a (piece of pretty cloth) _____ that is on a chair.

Later in the story, the young man says he plans to leave before Saturday. Henry is (very unhappy) _____ because he wants the young man to meet his wife. Henry (waits for) _____ his wife to come home on Saturday. The young man sees a photograph of Henry's wife and decides to stay.

Henry's friends come to visit. When Henry reads them a letter from his wife, the men have (drops of water) _____ in their eyes.

At the end of the story, the young man learns about the wife's (failure to return home) _____. He is surprised to hear that this happened 19 years ago. Henry's friends tell the young man that every year on the (date) _____ of this event, Henry's friends help him to (have a party for) _____ her return.

3. Grammar: Simple Present and Present Continuous Verb Tenses

Two present verb tense forms in English are the *simple present* and the *present continuous*.

▢ **The simple present is used when a thing or an action is true or repeated. Words and phrases like *every day, every year, always, often, usually, sometimes,* or *never* can be used to show the simple present.**

To make the simple present for singular subjects or the pronouns *he, she,* or *it,* add *-s, -es,* or *-ies* to the end of the main verb.

Examples:
Henry tries to keep his cottage clean.
Henry misses his wife.
Every day, Henry waits for his wife.

To make the simple present for plural subjects or the pronouns *I, you, we,* or *they,* do not add anything to the end of the main verb.

Examples:
Henry's friends decorate his house with flowers every year.
Tom, Joe, and Charley keep Henry company.
They stay with him all night.

The present continuous is used when an action is happening right now. Words like *now*, *right now*, or *at this moment* can be used to show the present continuous.

To make the present continuous, use *is*, *am*, or *are* (forms of the auxiliary verb "be") and the *-ing* form of the main verb.

Examples:

Right now, Henry is waiting for his wife.
His friends are waiting with him.
I am waiting, too.

■ *Practice 1*

Look at the following sentences. In the chart next to the sentences, check ✓ *simple present* or *present continuous* for the verbs in **bold**.

	simple present	present continuous
1. The young man **is looking** for gold today.	____	✓
2. In the story, the young man **meets** Henry.	____	____
3. Henry and the young man **go** into the cottage.	____	____
4. Henry **is showing** the young man his wife's picture now.	____	____
5. He **asks** the young man to stay and meet his wife.	____	____
6. The young man **decides** to stay until Saturday.	____	____
7. Now a neighbor **is reading** a letter from Henry's wife.	____	____
8. Some friends always **visit** Henry at this time of year.	____	____
9. Henry **waits** for his wife every day.	____	____
10. The men **are celebrating** at Henry's house at this moment.	____	____

■ *Practice 2*

In the following sentences, look at the underlined verb or verbs. If the verb form is correct, put a check ✓ next to the sentence. If the verb form is incorrect, write the correct sentence on the blank line.

1. Every anniversary, Henry's friends <u>are staying</u> with him.

   Every anniversary, Henry's friends stay with him.

2. They <u>decorate</u> his house for him.

   _____

3. Right now, the men <u>come</u> to Henry's house.

   _____

4. The men always <u>stay</u> with Henry all night.

   _____

5. Everyone usually <u>is singing</u> songs.

   _____

6. Henry often <u>falls</u> asleep during the celebration.

   _____

7. When he wakes up, Henry <u>is</u> always <u>remembering</u> his lovely wife.

   _____

8. All the men <u>are missing</u> Henry's wife.

   _____

1. Sharing Ideas

With a partner or in a small group, discuss the following questions.

1. In the beginning of the story, did you notice anything strange about Henry's behavior? Explain your answer.
2. Why does the young man decide to stay and meet Henry's wife?
3. Does the friendship of the other men help or hurt Henry? Why or why not?
4. What do you think happened to Henry's wife? Why didn't she return home?

2. Reading Between the Lines

Authors often write something that can have more than one meaning. You need to figure out what the author means. This is called *reading between the lines*. Read the following sentences from the story. Then circle the answer that shows the author's meaning. If you need help, look back at the story. Discuss your answers.

1. I watched him smooth a scarf which lay over the arm of a chair. It was like the pats a mother gives a child after she combs and brushes the child's hair.

   a. Henry smoothed the scarf the way a mother smoothes her child's hair.

   b. Henry loved and missed his wife.

   c. Henry thought his house needed to be cleaned.

2. Henry looked at me, and then he looked at a small photo sitting on a shelf.

   a. Henry did not want to look at the young man anymore.

   b. Henry wanted the young man to notice the photo.

   c. Henry wanted the young man to leave.

3. Once again, Henry read her letter, and once again I saw tears in another old man's eyes.

   a. Something about the letter made the old men cry.

   b. Another old man had something in his eyes.

   c. Henry read the letter too many times, and the old men were bored.

3. Analyzing the Story: Surprise Ending

As you read on page 90, many stories have *surprise endings*. If you read the story again, you will see that some sentences in the story give clues about the ending. Put a check ✓ next to the sentences below that are clues. Put an X next to the sentences that are not clues.

Sentences from the Story	Clues	Not Clues
The cottage was decorated with a woman's touch. There were pictures hanging on the walls and rugs on the floors. There were books, vases, and other pretty decorations.		X
"Yes, she was nineteen on her last birthday."		
"Tom, you are doing it again. Take your hands away from your eyes. You always do that when I read a letter from her."		
Four times Henry walked up the road and looked for her. "I'm worried," he said. "I know she's not due until nine o'clock, but maybe something happened. You don't think anything happened, do you?"		

4. Summary

Put the following sentences in the correct order to summarize the story. Write the numbers 1 to 6 to show the order. The first one has been done for you.

_____ Henry is waiting for his wife to return from a visit to her family.

_____ Each neighbor drops by to see when she will return.

_____ Henry reads a letter from his wife, and the neighbors cry.

_____ Henry shows the young man a picture of his wife.

_____ The young man learns that Henry's wife disappeared 19 years ago.

___1___ Henry invites the young man to come into his cozy cottage.

5. Writing

Pretend you are Henry's young wife. Write a letter telling him what you are doing now and what you do every day while visiting your family. Use the present verb tenses.

Chapter 8

The Mask of the Red Death EDGAR ALLAN POE

PRE-READING

1. Think Before You Read

Answer the following questions.

1. What are some reasons people wear costumes?
2. Have you ever worn a costume to a party? Describe or draw the costume.
3. Have you ever seen someone wearing a mask? Was it scary?

2. Picture Focus

With a partner, talk about the picture.

Why do you think the people in the picture are wearing costumes?

3. Key Vocabulary

Study the following key words from the story. They all relate to *scary stories*. Then complete the paragraph using each word once.

> **victims** people who are hurt or killed by something
>
> **suffered** experienced something bad
>
> **blood** the red liquid that flows through our bodies
>
> **flames** the hot light of a fire
>
> **horror** producing a strong feeling of fear
>
> **grave** a place where a dead person is buried under the ground

A lot of people enjoy _____ stories or movies. These stories usually tell how some people become _____ of a terrible event. We learn how the people _____, and we might see a lot of _____. Sometimes, dead people come back from the _____. It is fun to read scary stories or watch scary movies at night, especially when the _____ of a fireplace or a candle are the only light around us.

4. Story Preview 🎧

Read the preview of the story. Then answer the question in *Making Predictions* on the next page.

> The Red Death is a terrible disease. It kills half the people in Prince Prospero's country. To avoid getting the disease, the Prince invites a thousand friends and some entertainers to stay with him in his castle. Then he locks the doors and leaves people outside the castle to die. After a few months, the prince decides to have a masquerade or costume party for his guests.

5. Making Predictions

From the *Story Preview* try to predict what will happen. Circle one choice below or write your own answer. Discuss your prediction with a partner.

What will happen at the masquerade party?

1. The prince will fall in love with someone wearing a mask.

2. An uninvited guest will come to the party.

3. The prince will let all the people of his country into the castle.

4. _____

6. Idioms and Expressions

You will find these idioms and expressions in the story.

---

sharp pains a strong, sudden bad feeling in the body

wild and scary causing fear; frightening

the clock struck when a clock made a musical sound (chime)

made fun of treated someone or something like a joke

How dare you? an angry question asked when someone acts or speaks
   very impolitely

gained courage became brave

like a thief in the night a sudden, unexpected appearance or event

---

7. Literary Term: Atmosphere

Atmosphere is the feelings or mood a story creates. The author often uses the setting or events to create a pleasant or unpleasant atmosphere. Edgar Allan Poe usually created a feeling of fear in his stories.

Focus   As you read the story, notice how the setting and events make you feel. Do your feelings change from the beginning to the ending of the story? Do your feelings remain the same throughout the story?

About the Author

Edgar Allan Poe (1809–1849) was born in Boston, Massachusetts. Both of his parents were actors. They died when Poe was only two years old. A wealthy man named John Allan took the child into his home in Richmond, Virginia. Poe took Allan's last name as his middle name. At first, Allan gave Poe a comfortable life and a good education. Later, Allan and Poe had a fight and never saw each other again.

Poe worked as a writer and editor for newspapers and magazines. He also wrote books of poetry. Poe is most famous for his short stories of mystery and horror. Some of his famous short stories are "The Tell-Tale Heart," "The Black Cat," and the story you are about to read, "The Mask of the Red Death."

Poe died in Baltimore, Maryland, at the age of 40. No one knows exactly what happened to him. The cause of Poe's death remains a big mystery.

The Mask of the Red Death

Audio starts at line 26

The Red Death was a terrible disease. Its victims suffered sharp pains, felt dizzy, and their faces had spots of blood. People died within a half hour. 5 Half the people in Prince Prospero's country were dead.

Everyone was frightened except the prince. He was happy because he had a plan. He took a thousand friends, both men and women, to stay with 10 him in his big castle. He invited actors, singers, dancers, musicians, clowns, and other men and women to entertain his guests. He put all kinds of delicious food in the kitchen. There 15 was enough food to feed everybody for years.

The castle had a tall stone wall around it and strong iron gates. The prince locked the gates. No one could 20 leave, and no one could enter. Nobody cared about the people dying outside the castle walls. Everybody inside the castle was safe. Outside was the Red Death. 25

Toward the end of the fifth or sixth

month, Prince Prospero decided to have a large party for his thousand friends. It was a very colorful and elegant masked ball. Everyone wore strange, wild costumes and masks.

But first, let me tell you about the rooms where the party was held in this marvelous castle. There were seven rooms, every one in a different color. The walls and decorations in six of the rooms matched the color of the glass in the windows. The first room and window were all blue. The second was purple. The third room was green; the fourth, orange; the fifth, white; and the sixth, violet. The seventh room was different. Everything was black except the window. The glass of that window was red, the color of blood.

There were no lights in any of the rooms. Instead, a fire burned outside each window. The flames from the fire made the color of the glass dance around inside each room. But the firelight through the blood-red window made the black room look wild and scary. No one wanted to enter.

In this room sat a very large black clock. Every sixty minutes, the clock struck the hour. The sound of the chimes was so strange that the musicians stopped their music and the dancers stood still. The guests became pale and quiet, but only for a minute. As soon as the chimes finished, the noise and laughter began again.

And so, the party continued until midnight. At this hour, the clock sounded twelve times. Just then, many of the guests noticed a masked stranger. He walked slowly among the dancers. Fear and worry spread through the room. People whispered in horror.

His costume made fun of something that no one dared make fun of. He was tall and thin and dressed from head to foot in a white sheet. He was ready for the grave. His mask looked like a dead man's face. His costume and his face also had red spots – he was dressed as the Red Death.

The horrified prince spoke to him angrily, "How dare you wear this costume of death?"

Then the prince told his servants, "Grab him and take off his mask. We want to know who we will hang when the sun rises tomorrow."

The prince stood in the blue room when he said these words. At first, some of the crowd rushed toward the stranger, but nobody wanted to touch him. The stranger passed the prince and walked through the blue room to the purple – through the purple to the green – through the green to the orange – through the orange again to the white – and even to the violet room before anyone tried to stop him. It was then, however, that the prince angrily rushed through the six rooms. No one followed him. They were all afraid. The prince, who carried a dagger,[1] followed the figure into the black room. Suddenly, the stranger turned and looked at the prince. Instantly, Prince Prospero cried out, dropped the dagger, and fell to the floor dead.

[1] *dagger*: a short knife

Then, some of the guests gained courage and rushed forward. They grabbed the tall masked figure as he stood in front of the black clock. But, in horror, they found there was no human form under the sheet and mask.

Suddenly, the stranger turned and looked at the prince. Instantly, Prince Prospero cried out, dropped the dagger, and fell to the floor dead.

At that moment they knew the stranger was the Red Death. He came like a thief in the night. One by one, each guest fell dead. The life of the black clock went out with the death of the last guest. And the flames of the fires died as well. The Red Death ruled over all.

1. Understanding the Story

With a partner or in a small group, discuss the following questions.

1. What is the Red Death?
2. What is Prince Prospero's plan?
3. How does the prince entertain his guests?
4. What is different about the black room?
5. Who is the stranger that comes to the party? How is he dressed?

2. Vocabulary Comprehension

The words on the left are in the story. Match each word to the correct definition on the right. Write the letter of the definition on the blank line.

_e_	1. dizzy	a.	doors in an outside fence or wall
___	2. frightened	b.	a large, royal home that is protected with stone walls
___	3. castle	c.	kill someone by placing a rope around the neck
___	4. entertain	d.	a large piece of cloth used to cover a bed
___	5. gates	e.	feeling like everything is turning around and you might fall
___	6. marvelous		
___	7. sheet	f.	controlled a group of people or a country
___	8. horrified	g.	take hold of
___	9. grab	h.	feeling fear; scared
___	10. hang	i.	surprised in a bad way
___	11. rushed	j.	wonderful; very good
___	12. ruled	k.	ran quickly
		l.	give someone an enjoyable time

3. Grammar: The Simple Past Tense and Regular and Irregular Verb Forms

The *simple past* tense shows that an action happened in the past and is finished. In English, the simple past is formed by changing *regular verbs* and *irregular verbs*.

■ To make the simple past of regular verbs, add *-d* or *-ed* to the end.

Examples:

invite → invited   rush → rushed   suffer → suffered

When a verb ends in *y* and *y* is a vowel sound, change *y* to *i* and add *-ed.*

Examples:

carry → carried   cry → cried   try → tried

When a verb has a short vowel followed by a consonant, double the consonant.

Examples:

drop → dropped   grab → grabbed   stop → stopped

■ To make the simple past of irregular verbs, you must memorize their forms. Note that some irregular verbs have the same form in the present and past tenses.

Examples:

is / am / are → was / were
have / has → had

begin → began	come → came	go → went
know → knew	make → made	say → said
strike → struck	take → took	wear → wore
put → put	spread → spread	

■ *Practice 1*

The following paragraph from the story has seven regular past verbs and seven irregular past verbs. Underline the regular past verbs once and the irregular past verbs twice.

In this room sat a very large black clock. Every sixty minutes, the clock struck the hour. The sound of the chimes was so strange that the musicians stopped their music and the dancers stood still. The guests became pale and quiet, but only for a minute. As soon as the chimes finished, the noise and laughter began again. And so, the party continued until midnight. At this hour, the clock sounded twelve times. Just then, many of the guests noticed a masked stranger. He walked slowly among the dancers. Fear and worry spread through the rooms. People whispered in horror.

■ *Practice 2*

The following sentences are about the story. Complete each sentence with the correct past tense form of the verb in parentheses.

1. Prince Prospero _____ (rule) the country from his marvelous castle.

2. There _____ (be) a terrible disease in the country.

3. Many people _____ (die) from the disease.

4. Prince Prospero _____ (take) a thousand people into his castle.

5. Prince Prospero _____ (decide) to have a party.

6. At first, the people _____ (have) a good time at the party.

7. Then a stranger _____ (come) to the party.

8. The people _____ (whisper) in fear.

9. They _____ (grab) the stranger.

10. Then, the people in the castle _____ (fall) dead from the Red Death.

D | THINKING ABOUT THE STORY

1. Sharing Ideas

With a partner or in a small group, discuss the following questions.

1. Why does the prince think he is safe from the Red Death?
2. What kinds of people do you think were left outside the castle to die?
3. Why does most of the action happen in the seventh room?
4. How do you think the Red Death came into the castle?
5. Do you feel sorry for the prince? Why or why not?

2. Reading Between the Lines

Authors often write something that can have more than one meaning. You need to figure out what the author means. This is called *reading between the lines*. Read the following sentences from the story. Then circle the answer that shows the author's meaning. If you need help, look back at the story. Discuss your answers.

1. There was enough food to feed everybody for years.

    a. The prince's farms produced a lot of food.

    b. The prince wanted to show how rich he was.

    c. The prince planned to stay inside the castle for a long time.

2. The sound of the chimes was so strange that the musicians stopped their music and the dancers stood still. The guests became pale and quiet, but only for a minute.

    a. The sound of the clock was too loud, and people couldn't hear the music.

    b. People were frightened when they heard the strange sound.

    c. The sound of the clock was like beautiful music.

3. His costume made fun of something that no one dared make fun of.

    a. Some things, like death, are too serious to joke about.

    b. His costume was the funniest one of all.

    c. Everyone thought he had the best costume.

4. The Red Death ruled over all.

    a. The Red Death moved into Prince Prospero's castle.

    b. The Red Death was more powerful than anyone.

    c. The Red Death opened up the gates of the castle.

3. Analyzing the Story: Atmosphere

As you read on page 102, the *atmosphere* of a story makes you feel something pleasant or unpleasant. "The Mask of the Red Death" makes the reader feel fear. Read the story again. What things or events made this a scary story for you? Write those items in the chart. One example that may have been scary to you is already in the chart.

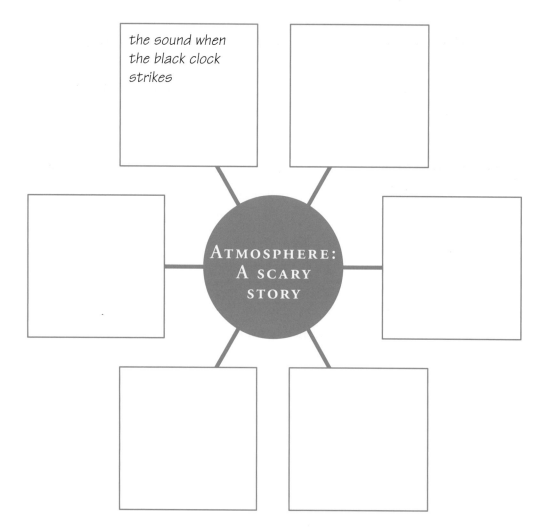

the sound when the black clock strikes

ATMOSPHERE: A SCARY STORY

4. Summary

Put the following sentences in the correct order to summarize the story. Write the numbers 1 to 8 to show the order. The first one has been done for you.

_____ Everyone in the castle dies.

_____ Prince Prospero entertains his guests at a costume party.

_____ The windows in the seventh room are the color of blood.

___1___ To escape the Red Death, Prince Prospero takes a thousand friends to his castle.

_____ When the guests grab the stranger, they find nothing under the sheet.

_____ Prince Prospero falls to the floor dead.

_____ The guests see a stranger dressed in a white sheet and mask with red spots.

_____ The prince locks the gates of the castle to keep out the Red Death.

5. Writing

Imagine you were a guest at Prince Prospero's party. Describe how you felt as the clock struck midnight.

Chapter 9
The Legend of Sleepy Hollow WASHINGTON IRVING

A PRE-READING

1. Think Before You Read

Answer the following questions.

1. What does the word *legend* mean?
2. What are some legends from your culture? Explain one legend.
3. Do you believe legends can be true? Why or why not?

2. Picture Focus

With a partner, talk about the picture.

Why does the man look frightened?

3. Key Vocabulary

Study the following key words from the story. They all relate to *the supernatural*. Then complete the paragraph using each word once.

> **superstitious** believing that certain things will bring bad luck
>
> **ghosts** the spirits of dead people that visit living people
>
> **haunt** appear somewhere, often in the form of a ghost
>
> **tales** stories that are invented or hard to believe
>
> **mysterious** describing something that cannot be explained

The supernatural cannot be explained by our knowledge of science. However, some people believe in supernatural events. These people are very

_____. They may believe that legends and strange

_____ are true. In some cultures, people think that any Friday that

is on the thirteenth day of a month is an unlucky day. Other cultures think that if

they see the number 4, they will die. Some people also believe in

_____. They think that the spirits of the dead _____

certain places around us. Maybe these people read too many scary stories about

_____ events.

4. Story Preview 🎧

Read the preview of the story. Then answer the question in *Making Predictions* on the next page.

> The people of Sleepy Hollow are superstitious. They believe in ghosts, especially one they call the Headless Horseman. This ghost rides through the village at midnight looking for his head. Most of the townspeople are afraid of him, including Ichabod Crane, the village school teacher.

5. Making Predictions

From the *Story Preview*, try to predict what will happen. Circle one choice below or write your own answer. Discuss your prediction with a partner.

What will happen if Ichabod Crane meets the ghost?

1. Ichabod will try to kill the ghost.

2. Ichabod will leave Sleepy Hollow.

3. Ichabod will help the ghost find his head.

4. _____

6. Idioms and Expressions

You will find these idioms and expressions in the story.

---

play tricks on make another person the victim of a joke or bad event

feasting on enjoying a lot of good food

mouth watering looks so good you can't wait to eat it

broke up ended an event or a relationship

marriage proposal the time when a person asks someone to marry him or her

goose bumps small bumps that cover the skin when someone is frightened or cold

---

7. Literary Term: Foreshadowing

Foreshadowing is when an author gives you clues about what is going to happen in the story. You can find the clues easily as you read the story. In *surprise endings* (see Chapter 7, page 90), you often can't find the clues about the ending until you read the story a second time. Authors often use foreshadowing for mysteries and horror stories.

Focus   As you read the story, look for clues about what is going to happen to the main character, Ichabod Crane.

About the Author

Washington Irving (1783–1859) was born in New York City. He studied law for a short time, and then he decided to become a writer. He had success with his first book, *A History of New York*. About the same time, he became engaged to Matilda Hoffman. She died suddenly, and Irving was so sad that he never married. He went to Europe to forget the death of his fiancée, and he decided to live in Spain. In 1826, Irving went to work at the U.S. embassy in Madrid. In Europe, Irving wrote and published *The Sketch Book*. This book introduced the character Ichabod Crane in the story "The Legend of Sleepy Hollow."

Washington Irving later returned to the United States. He spent the rest of his life in Tarrytown, New York. There he built a home. He called it "Sunnyside." The house is now a museum dedicated to the memory of Washington Irving.

The Legend of Sleepy Hollow

Audio starts at line 124

Many years ago, there was a little town in the green valleys of the state of New York. The place was called Sleepy Hollow.

The people in this quiet village were very superstitious. They believed in ghosts. One particular ghost haunted the countryside. It was a ghost riding on a horse, and the ghost did not have a head on its body. People said it was the ghost of a soldier from the Revolutionary War.[1] The soldier's head was shot off by a cannon ball.

So everyone called the ghost "The Headless Horseman of Sleepy Hollow." People said the soldier was buried in one of the graves at the church. They believed the Horseman

[1] *Revolutionary War*: the war in the 1700s that was fought between the American Colonies and England and that led to the colonies becoming the United States of America

rode to the battlefield every night, looking for his head.

There was only one teacher in Sleepy Hollow. His name was Ichabod Crane. He was not a good-looking man. He was very tall and thin. His head was small, but his ears were large and his nose was long. Ichabod loved to eat. He didn't get much money working as a teacher, so he was always looking for a good meal. People often invited him to dinner. The women liked his good manners. He was a good source of news, and he taught singing.

Ichabod liked stories of ghosts. He enjoyed visiting the old women in the village. They passed many evenings telling tales of ghosts. They told tales of haunted fields, haunted bridges, and haunted houses, and particularly of the Headless Horseman. Ichabod always had to walk home alone at night after hearing the scary stories.

Ichabod's other interest was young ladies. He was in love with pretty Katrina Van Tassel. She was the only daughter of a rich farmer. Ichabod decided to ask Katrina to marry him. However, another man, Brom Bones, wanted to marry her, too.

Brom was big and strong. He was a great horse rider. He liked to play tricks on people he didn't like. Brom was also jealous. He soon noticed Ichabod's interest in Katrina. Bad feelings grew between Brom and Ichabod. Brom Bones boasted about what he would do to Ichabod Crane.

One fall day, when Ichabod was teaching, a man came to the schoolhouse with a letter. It was an invitation to a party at Van Tassel's farm. Ichabod was very excited. He

■   ■   ■

They passed many evenings telling tales of ghosts. They told tales of haunted fields, haunted bridges, and haunted houses, and particularly of the Headless Horseman.

■   ■   ■

quickly gave the students their lessons. He let them go home an hour early. Then he brushed his best coat and combed his hair. He borrowed an old horse and a saddle from Mr. Hans Van Ripper, to ride to the party.

It was evening when Ichabod arrived at Van Tassel's home. Everyone was feasting on all kinds of mouth-watering food. Ichabod was very happy while he was eating. He was thinking about the riches of Van Tassel's farm. He was thinking about asking Katrina to marry him. He was sure she would say yes. Then he would have a beautiful wife and Van Tassel's farm.

Brom Bones was also at the party. He came on his favorite horse – an animal known for its speed. Brom was boasting about his horse when Ichabod came in.

A musician began to play. Soon people were dancing. Ichabod was dancing with Katrina. Ichabod was as proud of his dancing as he was of his singing. Brom Bones was watching jealously from the corner.

When the dance ended, Ichabod joined a group of older men and women. They were telling stories about ghosts and strange events. The stories turned to their favorite ghost – the Headless Horseman. They said that every night, the Horseman tied his horse to a tree among the graves at the church.

The men and women were also talking about Old Brouwer, a farmer who said he didn't believe in ghosts. One night, Brouwer met the Horseman on the road. The Horseman made Brouwer get on his horse behind him and ride with him. At the bridge next to the church, the Horseman threw Brouwer into the small river. With the sound of thunder, the Horseman rode off over the treetops. Brom boasted that one time he had a race with the ghost, and Brom almost won.

The party gradually broke up. The old farmers took their families home. The younger people, with their arms around each other, began to leave. Ichabod stayed behind to make his marriage proposal. But something must have gone wrong because a few minutes later, Ichabod ran out the front door of Van Tassel's home, ran straight to his horse, and rode toward his own home. The time was midnight.

The night grew darker. Ichabod thought of the stories about the Headless Horseman. He was coming to the wooden bridge when suddenly, he saw something large and black. Goose bumps covered Ichabod's body, and the hair on his head rose in fear. The figure had no head! It was the horseman, and he was carrying his head on his saddle. Ichabod kicked his horse to make it go faster, but the Headless Horseman rode right behind Ichabod.

Ichabod was not a good rider. The saddle became loose, and it fell to the ground. In his terror, Ichabod grabbed his horse's neck. If only he could get across the bridge! At that moment, the ghost took his head and threw it at Ichabod. The head hit Ichabod and knocked him off his horse.

The next morning, Van Ripper found his horse without its saddle. Ichabod did not appear at breakfast. The boys came to the school, but there was no teacher. Dinner time came, but where was Ichabod?

On the road someone found the saddle. On the wooden bridge were Ichabod Crane's hat and a broken pumpkin. The farmers searched the small river, but Ichabod's body was never found.

The mysterious event caused much talk among the people of Sleepy Hollow. They were sure that the Headless Horsemen carried Ichabod Crane away.

Several years later, a farmer from Sleepy Hollow visited New York City. He came back with the news that Ichabod Crane was alive. Ichabod said he left Sleepy Hollow out of fear of the ghost and because he was disappointed in love. Ichabod did well in the city. He became a lawyer, then a politician, and finally a judge.

Meanwhile, Brom Bones married Katrina Van Tassel. Brom always enjoyed hearing the story of Ichabod Crane. He laughed loudly every time someone mentioned the pumpkin.

The old country women, however, still believe that the ghost took Ichabod away on his midnight ride in Sleepy Hollow. People grew even more superstitious about the bridge. They moved the road to the church to avoid the bridge, and they no longer used the old schoolhouse. Some people reported that the ghost of the unfortunate teacher haunted the empty schoolhouse. Others imagine hearing him singing in the peaceful valleys around Sleepy Hollow.

1. Understanding the Story

With a partner or in a small group, discuss the following questions.

1. What do the people of Sleepy Hollow believe about the Headless Horseman?
2. What kind of man is Ichabod Crane? Describe him.
3. Why is Ichabod so happy to receive an invitation to the party at Van Tassel's home?
4. Why is Brom Bones jealous of Ichabod Crane?
5. What happens to Ichabod after he leaves the party at Van Tassel's farm?

2. Vocabulary Comprehension

The words in the list are in the story. Find the words in the story, and try to understand their meanings. Then complete the sentences with words in the list. Use each word once.

valley	soldier	buried	manners
boast	borrow	saddle	jealous
thunder	loose	pumpkin	search

1. Brom Bones liked to _____*boast*_____ about himself. He said he was the best at everything.

2. Ichabod Crane didn't have a horse. He had to _____ one.

3. Brom Bones was _____ of Ichabod Crane. Brom wanted to marry Katrina.

4. Ichabod also needed a _____ for the horse.

5. Everyone liked to invite Ichabod for dinner because he had nice _____.

6. Sleepy Hollow was in a beautiful _____ in the state of New York.

7. On the bridge, the men found a big orange _____. It was broken.

8. People said the Headless Horseman was the ghost of a _____.

9. The body was _____ in a grave near the church.

10. People heard _____ when the Headless Horseman flew over the trees.

11. The townspeople decided to _____ in the small river for Ichabod's body.

12. The saddle was _____ on the horse. Ichabod had to grab the horse's neck.

3. *Grammar: Simple Past and Past Continuous Verb Tenses*

Both the *simple past tense* and the *past continuous tense* are used for actions in the past. In Chapter 8 (page 107), you learned that the simple past is used for an action that happened in the past and is finished.

> **The past continuous is used for an action in the past that is taking place just before another action in the past begins. We often use it in the same sentence as the simple past.**

To make the past continuous verb tense, use *was* or *were* + the *-ing* form of the main verb.

Example:

PAST CONTINUOUS   SIMPLE PAST

One fall day, while Ichabod was teaching, a man came to the schoolhouse with a letter.

> **Some verbs are not usually used in the past continuous form.**

Examples:

know	want	need	like	hear
love	hate	seem	believe	

■ *Practice 1*

The following sentences are about the story. Circle the correct verb or verbs in parentheses to complete each sentence.

1. Ichabod (was planning / planning) to ask Katrina to marry him.

2. A lot of people (was dancing / were dancing) at the party.

3. Brom Bones (was watching / watching) while Ichabod (dance / was dancing) with Katrina.

4. Brom often (boasted / boasting) about what he (want / wanted) to do to Ichabod.

5. Katrina (was making / was made) Brom jealous.

6. Ichabod (went / going) to sit with some of the old men and women. The older people (were telling / was telling) ghost stories.

■ Practice 2

Read the following conversation between two women in Sleepy Hollow. Next to each sentence in the chart, check ✓ *simple past* or *past continuous* for the verbs in **bold**.

	simple past	past continuous
Anna comes to Betty's house.		
Anna: Hello, Betty. What **were** you **doing**?	____	✓
Betty: I **was cooking** dinner.	____	____
Anna: What **were** you **making**?	____	____
Betty: Soup. My brother **sent** me a chicken from his farm.	____	____
Anna: **Did** you **hear** the news?	____	____
Betty: What news? Nobody **told** me anything.	____	____
Anna: A horseman without a head **was riding** through town	____	____
last night, and someone **saw** him!	____	____
Betty: What **did** you **say**? No head? On a horse?	____	____
Was someone **imagining** things?	____	____
Anna: Well, old Brouwer **was walking** home last night when	____	____
the headless man **rode** by on his big, black horse.	____	____
Betty: So what **happened**?	____	____
Anna: The ghost **made** Brouwer get up on his horse!	____	____
Betty: But old Brouwer never **believed** in ghosts.	____	____
Anna: Well, he **changed** his mind last night!	____	____

THINKING ABOUT THE STORY

1. Sharing Ideas

With a partner or in a small group, discuss the following questions.

1. Do you like Ichabod Crane? Why or why not?
2. Do you like Brom Bones? Why is he important in the story? Explain your answers.
3. Why does everyone fear the Headless Horseman?
4. What do you think happened when Ichabod asked Katrina to marry him?
5. Why do you think the people of Sleepy Hollow found a pumpkin on the wooden bridge?

2. Reading Between the Lines

Authors often write something that can have more than one meaning. You need to figure out what the author means. This is called *reading between the lines*. Read the following sentences from the story. Then circle the answer that shows the author's meaning. If you need help, look back at the story. Discuss your answers.

1. He [Brom Bones] liked to play tricks on people he didn't like.

   a. Brom Bones was a funny person.

   b. Brom Bones loved Katrina.

   c. Brom Bones didn't like Ichabod.

2. . . . suddenly, he saw something large and black.

   a. It was the Headless Horseman.

   b. It was a large tree.

   c. It was the bridge over the stream.

3. Brom always enjoyed hearing the story of Ichabod Crane. He laughed loudly every time someone mentioned the pumpkin.

   a. Brom didn't believe the story.

   b. Brom knew a secret about the pumpkin.

   c. Brom was glad that Ichabod left the village.

3. Analyzing the Story: Foreshadowing

As you read on page 114, *foreshadowing* is when an author gives clues about what is going to happen in the story. The end of "The Legend of Sleepy Hollow" is summarized in the box on the right. Find examples of foreshadowing in the story that help predict the ending. Find one example for each set of lines from the story. Put the examples in the boxes on the left.

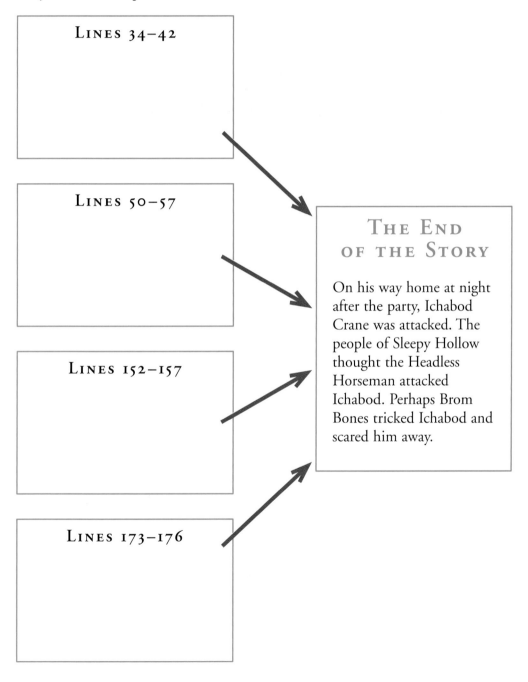

LINES 34–42

LINES 50–57

LINES 152–157

LINES 173–176

THE END OF THE STORY

On his way home at night after the party, Ichabod Crane was attacked. The people of Sleepy Hollow thought the Headless Horseman attacked Ichabod. Perhaps Brom Bones tricked Ichabod and scared him away.

4. Summary

Put the following sentences in the correct order to summarize the story. Write the numbers 1 to 8 to show the order. The first one has been done for you.

_____ Ichabod Crane receives an invitation to Van Tassel's party.

_____ Ichabod's hat and a broken pumpkin are found on the wooden bridge.

___1___ The people of Sleepy Hollow believe in ghosts.

_____ The Headless Horseman chases Ichabod and knocks him off his horse.

_____ Brom Bones marries Katrina.

_____ People say the Headless Horseman is the ghost of a soldier.

_____ At midnight, Ichabod leaves the party after something goes wrong.

_____ Ichabod makes Brom Bones jealous.

5. Writing

Write a paragraph that explains what you think really happened at the end of "The Legend of Sleepy Hollow." It could be one of the following endings or your own choice.

• Ichabod ran away to New York City and became a judge.

• The Headless Horseman carried Ichabod Crane away.

• Brom Bones played a trick on Ichabod and scared him away.

• _____

Summing Up

A TAKE A CLOSER LOOK

1. Theme Comparison: Mystery and Fantasy

Life is full of mysteries. There are many things we can't explain, especially when we are lonely or frightened. In the first story of Part Three, a lonely man believes that his missing wife will return by Saturday night. In the second story, a mysterious guest at a masquerade party turns out to be death. At the end of the last story, we wonder what really happened to Ichabod Crane.

With a partner, discuss the following questions.

1. If you could ask Mark Twain one question about Henry and his wife's disappearance, what would you ask?
2. What does Edgar Allan Poe want us to think about death?
3. Which ending of "The Legend of Sleepy Hollow" do you think Washington Irving wants us to believe?

2. Freewriting

Write the word *mystery* at the top of a sheet of paper. Then write any words that come into your mind when you think of *mystery*. For 15 minutes, write about a mysterious event from a movie, a book, or your own life. What was the situation? Where did it take place? Who was in the event? Did the event frighten you? Was the mystery finally solved?

B REVIEW

1. Grammar Review

Circle the correct verb or verbs in parentheses to complete the following sentences.

1. I (go / am going / went / was going) to scary movies every Friday night.

2. Last Friday night, I (see / saw / am seeing / was seeing) a really scary movie.

3. My friends (come / was coming / are coming / came) with me.

4. While we (watched / watch / are watching / were watching) the movie, the lights (are turning / were turning / turned / turn) off.

5. Everyone in the theater (began / was beginning / is beginning / begins) to scream.

6. My friend Ichabod (drops / dropped / was dropping / is dropping) his popcorn while everyone (is screaming / screams / screamed / was screaming).

7. Right now, I (wrote / am writing / was writing / write) about last Friday night in my journal.

8. Now I (think / was thinking / thought / am thinking) that night wasn't scary – it was funny.

2. Vocabulary Review

The words in the list are in the word search box. Find the words in the box. The words are written across or down.

blood	cottage	cozy	dizzy	grab	horror
human	invites	jealous	loose	manners	soldier
suffered	taste	tears	thunder	valley	victims

```
H A J E A L O U S L P M A N N E R S Q F O
U S I N V I T E S G G R A B W K A O I G B
M M I N A D E C C O T T A G E X B L O O D
A T Q W L T A S T E V I C T I M S D F H C
N Y I P L J R T H U N D E R Z Q D I Z Z Y
L O O S E B S U F F E R E D R E W E O E S
T C O Z Y Z D V K E S O H O R R O R T M U
```

Filling Out the Elements Chart

This chart shows the five basic elements of a short story. You can find definitions for these elements on page 170. Some of these elements have been filled out for "The Californian's Tale." Complete the chart. Then copy the blank chart on page xvii and fill it out for "The Mask of the Red Death" or "The Legend of Sleepy Hollow" or for both stories. Share your charts with a partner or in a small group.

Elements of _____ The Californian's Tale _____
(name of story)

SETTING

CHARACTERS

PLOT

CONFLICT
The conflict is between what we wish to believe and what is really true.

It can also be about telling someone the truth or letting them believe what they want to believe.

THEME(S)
Imagining and pretending something different from the truth.

Not believing a loved one has died.

Close
Relationships

From early childhood, we form close relationships with other people – our families, our classmates, our neighbors, our co-workers – and maybe we even fall in love with someone special. Some of these relationships make us very happy; others make us sad and disappointed. Through their characters, writers can help us understand relationships and how they make us feel.

 In the first story you are about to read, a young man's images of race and culture destroy the happiness of the woman he loves. In the second story, a family keeps secrets from each other. In the final story, the relationship between a mother and her son is tested. As you read each story, think about how you would feel in the relationships if you were the main character.

Chapter 12

All the Years of Her Life
– Morley Callaghan

Chapter 10

Its Wavering Image EDITH EATON

A PRE-READING

1. Think Before You Read

Answer the following questions.

1. Do you know anyone whose mother is from one race or culture and whose father is from another race or culture?
2. Do you think that a person from one race or culture should marry a person from another race or culture? Why or why not?
3. What advantages and disadvantages do you think that people of two races – biracial people – have? Explain your answer.

2. Picture Focus

With a partner, talk about the picture.

Why do you think the young woman looks angry?

3. Key Vocabulary

Study the following key words and expressions from the story. They all relate to *race* and *culture*. Then complete the paragraph using each word or expression once.

> **ethnicity** racial, national, or cultural background
>
> **facial features** eyes, nose, mouth, cheeks, and chin of a person
>
> **belong** be a part of a place or group
>
> **foreign** of a country or custom that is not the same as yours
>
> **customs** practices or habits of a person, group, or country
>
> **beliefs** ideas that a person or group believes are true

In today's world, it is not unusual to meet people who _____ to more than one race or one culture. When you meet them, it can be difficult to know their _____ just by looking at or talking with them. They may seem _____ to you even though they were born in the same country as you. For example, the person may have the _____ _____ from more than one race. In addition, because the person has grown up with parents from two different cultures, he or she may have an unusual combination of _____ and _____.

4. Story Preview 🎧

Read the preview of the story. Then answer the questions in *Making Predictions* on the next page.

> Pan is a half-white, half-Chinese girl. She lives with her Chinese father in Chinatown, in the Canadian city of Montreal. Her white mother is dead. Pan always feels comfortable with her father's people. She does not like to be with white people. That changes when Pan meets Mark Carson, a white journalist. They become friends, and then something happens between them.

5. Making Predictions

From the *Story Preview*, try to predict what will happen. Circle one choice below or write your own answer. Discuss your prediction with a partner.

What will happen as Pan and Mark become friends?

1. Pan will no longer be happy with Chinese people.

2. Pan and Mark will fall in love and get married.

3. Pan will decide she is not a white woman.

4. _____

6. Idioms and Expressions

You will find these idioms and expressions in the story.

---

sell one's soul do anything to get what one wants

shy away from avoid or stay away from something

at home with comfortable with

have no right not be allowed to do something

would rather prefer

Don't you dare! Never do that!

---

7. Literary Term: Conflict

Within a plot there is often a *conflict* or struggle. The conflict can be a fight or disagreement between characters, between characters and the environment, or inside a character's mind. Every story contains some type of conflict, and by the end of the story, the conflict ends.

Focus As you read the story, notice the conflict between the two main characters, Pan and Mark. What is their conflict? Also notice the conflict inside Pan's mind and how this conflict ends.

About the Author

Edith Eaton (1865–1914) was born to a Chinese mother and a British father. She grew up in a large family in Montreal, Quebec. While she was working as a typist, she began her career as a journalist. She wrote under the name Sui Sin Far. Her articles about the Chinese-Canadian community were published in several Montreal newspapers.

In the early 1900s, Eaton moved to the United States where she wrote about the Chinatowns in San Francisco, Seattle, and Boston. In 1912, she published her book of stories, *Mrs. Spring Fragrance*. "Its Wavering Image" is one of the stories.

Its Wavering Image

Audio starts at line 42

Pan was a half-white, half-Chinese girl. Her white mother was dead, so Pan lived alone with her Chinese father, Man Yu. Man Yu owned a
5 small shop on Du Pont Street in Montreal's Chinatown. All her life Pan lived in Chinatown. She never thought about being different until she met Mark Carson.
10 Mark Carson was a newspaper journalist. He was sent by his editor to write a story about life in Chinatown. He was a clever young man. He knew how to get people to tell him their
15 secrets. In fact, people who knew him said he was "a man who would sell his soul for a story."

First, Mark went to the shop of Man Yu. Pan was in the shop. She was helping her father. She always shied 20 away from white people. She was at home with her father's people. With her mother's, she felt strange.

When Mark first saw Pan, he wondered, "Is she Chinese, or white?" 25 He wasn't sure of her ethnicity. Her facial features were unusual. His editor told him, "She is an unusually smart girl. She can tell you more stories about the Chinese than any other 30 person in the city." For this reason, Mark became Pan's friend. He was also attracted to her.

Mark was Pan's first white friend. She took him everywhere in Chinatown. He was welcomed in clubs where only Chinese were allowed. Chinese groups invited him to their meetings. Everyone trusted him. Wherever he went with Pan, he was welcomed.

Soon, Pan and Mark fell in love. In the evenings, Pan took Mark up to her little apartment above her father's shop. They listened to a Chinese band playing music on the street below. Sometimes, her father would come up to ask if they wanted anything. Pan was proud of her father. She said, "I would rather have a Chinese for a father than a white one." Once, Mark asked, "Would you rather have a white man or a Chinese man for a husband?" For the first time, Pan did not have an answer.

One night, Mark took Pan's hand.

"Pan," he said, "you do not belong here. You are white!"

Pan cried out, "No, no."

"You are white," he repeated. "You have no right to be here."

"I was born here," she answered, "and the Chinese people see me as their own."

"But they do not understand you," he replied. "Your real self is foreign to them."

"They have an interest in me," Pan said. "Do not speak like that."

"But, I must. You have to decide what you will be – Chinese or white.

You can't be both."

A little Chinese boy brought them tea and cakes. He was a cute child. Mark laughed and played with him. Pan smiled.

When they were alone again, they looked out the window to see the first quarter of the moon shining on the river. It was a beautiful night. With his hand on Pan's shoulder, Mark began to sing:

And forever, and forever
As long as the river flows.
The moon and its changing
    reflection
Is a symbol of love
And its wavering image here.

Listening to the song, Pan began to cry. She was so happy.

"Look at me," Mark said, "Oh, Pan. These tears show that you are white."

Pan lifted her wet face. "Kiss me, Pan," Mark said. It was their first kiss.

The next morning, Mark began work on the special news article, which he promised his editor. Two days later, the article entitled, "Its Wavering Image" appeared in the newspaper.

Pan's father threw the paper at his daughter's feet and left the room. Surprised at her father's anger, Pan picked up the paper and read the words. "Betrayed!" she cried. Mark's article had every Chinese secret she told him. He made fun of Chinese customs and beliefs. He made fun of her friends and family. She looked at the title, "Its Wavering Image."

Mark was back in the city after being away for two months. He was excited. This evening he would see Pan again. He was sure she forgot about the article he wrote. However, he was a little worried as he climbed the hill to her father's shop. Why didn't Pan answer his letters when he was away?

When she opened the door, she was not smiling. Mark tried to explain about his article in the newspaper.

"I knew they would not blame you, Pan," he said.

Pan said nothing.

"And I never used your name."

Still, she did not answer.

Pan looked different. She was not herself tonight. He usually saw her in American clothes. Tonight, she wore a Chinese dress.

"Pan," he asked, "Why are you wearing that dress?"

"Because I am a Chinese woman," she answered.

"You are not!" Mark said. "You are a white woman. Your kiss promised me that."

"A white woman!" Pan answered. "Don't you dare call me a white woman! I will never be a white woman. You are a white man – and what is a promise to a white man?"

After Mark left, a little girl and her mother came to Man Yu's shop. Pan was sitting on a chair. She had angry tears in her eyes. The little girl put her head next to Pan's.

"Look," said the mother, "how my little girl loves you. Maybe you will have a child some day, and all this sadness will pass away."

And Pan, being a Chinese woman, was comforted.

1. Understanding the Story

With a partner or in a small group, discuss the following questions.

1. How does Pan meet Mark?
2. What does the newspaper editor tell Mark about Pan?
3. How does Pan help Mark learn about the people in Chinatown?
4. Why does Pan become angry with Mark?
5. At the end of the story, does Pan feel she is a white woman or a Chinese woman? Explain your answer.

2. Vocabulary Comprehension

The words in the list are in the story. Find the words in the story, and try to understand their meanings. Then answer the questions that follow the list. Use your own opinions, knowledge, or experiences.

journalist	welcomed	wavering	blame
editor	trusted	promised	comforted
clever	reflection	betrayed	
attracted	symbol	worried	

1. Do **editors** work only for newspapers?

   No. Some editors work for books or magazines.

2. When you are sad, what makes you feel the most **comforted**?

   _____

3. If you were a **journalist**, what types of stories would you write?

   _____

4. Have you ever **promised** someone something that you could not give them? Explain.

   _____

5. Are you **worried** about anything right now? What are you worried about?

_____

6. What is a **symbol** of love?

_____

7. When you pass a shop window, do you ever look at your **reflection** in the window? Why or why not?

_____

8. What type of person are you most **attracted** to?

_____

9. Have any of your friends or family ever **betrayed** you? What did they do?

_____

10. What is a **clever** way to save money?

_____

11. Are you **wavering** on any decision right now? What decision are you wavering on?

_____

12. Where have you felt the most **welcomed** in your life?

_____

13. Who should you **blame** if you are unhappy?

_____

14. Who is your most **trusted** friend? Why is he or she the most **trusted**?

_____

3. Grammar: Simple Sentences

A *simple sentence*, or an *independent clause*, is a complete thought. It has <u>one</u> *subject* and <u>one</u> *verb*. In English, the subject comes before the verb. Other words can help complete the thought.

- A subject is a noun or pronoun. It is the person or thing that performs the action of a verb. Words like *it* or *there* can also be subjects.

    Examples:
    Man Yu owned a small shop in Chinatown.
    The small shop was always busy.
    It sold food and other items.
    There were many people in the shop.

- A verb tells what the subject is or what the subject does.

    Examples:
    Pan was a half-white, half-Chinese girl.
    She lived in Chinatown.

- Other words can come before the subject or after the verb to complete the thought.

    Examples:
    Mark Carson was a newspaper journalist.
    Every day he wrote news articles.
    He wrote an article about the people of Chinatown.

- If a sentence has more than one clause, that is, it has more than one subject and one verb, it is a *complex sentence* (see page 150 for more on complex sentences).

    Examples:
    Mark was excited. (simple sentence)
    Mark was going to see Pan again. (simple sentence)
    Mark was excited because he was going to see Pan again.
      (complex sentence)

■ *Practice 1*

In the story, the author writes many short simple sentences. In the third paragraph, every sentence is a simple sentence. Read the paragraph again, and underline the subject and circle the verb in each sentence. Put *S* above the subject and *V* above the verb.

First, Mark went to the shop of Man Yu. Pan was in the shop. She was helping her father. She always shied away from white people. She was at home with her father's people. With her mother's, she felt strange.

■ *Practice 2*

The following sentences all come from the story. Some are simple sentences and some are complex sentences. Mark the simple sentences *SS* and the complex sentences *CX*.

_____ 1. She never thought about being different until she met Mark Carson.

_____ 2. Mark Carson was a newspaper journalist.

_____ 3. Wherever he went with Pan, he was welcomed.

_____ 4. For the first time, Pan did not have an answer.

_____ 5. A little Chinese boy brought them tea and cakes.

_____ 6. With his hand on Pan's shoulder, Mark began to sing.

_____ 7. He made fun of Chinese customs and beliefs.

_____ 8. When she opened the door, she was not smiling.

_____ 9. Tonight she wore a Chinese dress.

_____ 10. After Mark left, a little girl and her mother came to Man Yu's shop.

1. Sharing Ideas

With a partner or in a small group, discuss the following questions.

1. Why do you think Mark is attracted to Pan?
2. Why does Pan feel that Mark betrayed her?
3. What do you think Mark wants to happen when he comes back to see Pan?
4. Why does Mark want Pan to be white?
5. Why is the story titled "Its Wavering Image"? What are the wavering images in the story?

2. Reading Between the Lines

Authors often write something that can have more than one meaning. You need to figure out what the author means. This is called *reading between the lines*. Read the following sentences from the story. Then circle the answer that shows the author's meaning. If you need help, look back at the story. Discuss your answers.

1. . . . he was "a man who would sell his soul for a story."

   a. Mark loved to write stories.

   b. Mark would do anything he could to get a story.

   c. Mark didn't have a soul.

2. "Pan," he said, "You do not belong here. You are white!"

   a. Mark thinks that Man Yu isn't really Pan's father.

   b. Mark thinks the people of Chinatown do not like Pan.

   c. Mark thinks that Pan is more white than Chinese in her behavior.

3. Pan's father threw the paper at his daughter's feet and left the room.

   a. Pan's father didn't have time to read the paper.

   b. Pan's father was very angry about something in the paper.

   c. Pan's father finished reading the newspaper and had to leave quickly.

4. He usually saw her in American clothes. Tonight she wore a Chinese dress.

   a. Mark expected Pan to look and behave like a white woman.

   b. Mark thought Pan looked beautiful in her Chinese dress.

   c. Mark forgot what Pan looked like.

3. Analyzing the Story: Conflict

As you read on page 132, *conflict* can happen between people or inside the mind of one person. In this story, Pan's image of herself begins to waver when she meets Mark. The following diagram shows Pan's thoughts about her image from the beginning of the story to the end. Find the lines from the story for each thought. Write the line numbers in the blanks to complete the chart.

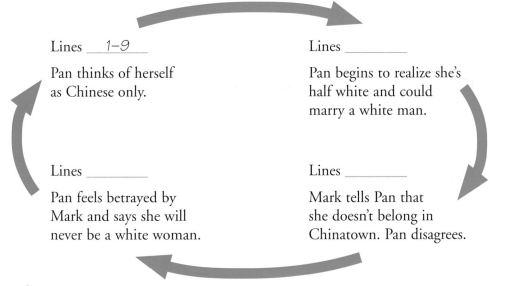

Lines ___1–9___

Pan thinks of herself as Chinese only.

Lines _____

Pan begins to realize she's half white and could marry a white man.

Lines _____

Pan feels betrayed by Mark and says she will never be a white woman.

Lines _____

Mark tells Pan that she doesn't belong in Chinatown. Pan disagrees.

4. Summary

Put the following sentences in the correct order to summarize the story. Write the numbers from 1 to 6 to show the order. The first one has been done for you.

_____ Mark's story makes fun of Chinese people and their culture.

_____ Mark and Pan fall in love.

___1___ Mark Carson wants to write an article about Chinatown.

_____ Mark meets Pan and wonders if she is Chinese or white.

_____ Pan feels betrayed by Mark and chooses to be Chinese, not white.

_____ Pan introduces Mark to her Chinese friends and takes him everywhere in Chinatown.

5. Writing

Pretend to be Mark. Write your thoughts as you walk home from your last visit with Pan.

Chapter 11

The Tree of Knowledge HENRY JAMES

1. Think Before You Read

Answer the following questions.

1. What does it mean to "keep a secret"?
2. Is it easy or difficult for you to keep a secret? Explain your answer.
3. What kind of secret should you keep? What kind of secret should you tell?

2. Picture Focus

With a partner, talk about the picture.

What is the relationship between the two men?

3. Key Vocabulary

Study the following key words from the story. They all relate to *the career of an artist*. Then complete the paragraph using each word once.

> **sculptor** artist who shapes art pieces out of wood, stone, metal, etc.
>
> **sculptures** pieces of art made out of wood, stone, metal, etc.
>
> **painters** artists who use oil, watercolors, or other types of paint to make pictures
>
> **famous** well known by many people
>
> **create** make new and original ideas and things
>
> **talent** special ability to do or make something
>
> **master** person who has great ability and experience to do something

The career of an artist is not easy. Artists must have both passion and

_____ for making art. They must be able to _____

art that other people will like. Some artists are _____ and use oil or

watercolors to make beautiful pictures. Other artists use wood, stone, or metal to

make interesting _____. This type of artist is called a

_____. To make money as an artist, artists must become

_____. If many people see their artwork and like it, they may buy

it. And people will pay more money for the art of a _____.

4. Story Preview 🎧

Read the preview of the story. Then answer the question in *Making Predictions* on the next page.

> Peter Brench is a single man. He is a very close friend to Mr. and Mrs. Mallow and their son Lance. Mr. Mallow is a sculptor. Lance wants to be an artist like his father. Mrs. Mallow also wants her son to be an artist, but Peter tries to discourage Lance. He thinks Lance should stay at Cambridge University to become a lawyer or banker. However, Lance decides to go to Paris to study art.

5. Making Predictions

From the *Story Preview*, try to predict what will happen. Circle one choice below or write your own answer. Discuss your prediction with a partner.

What will happen to Lance after he goes to Paris?

1. He will become a famous artist.

2. He will miss his family and come home.

3. He will learn something about his father, his mother, and Peter.

4. _____

6. Idioms and Expressions

You will find these idioms and expressions in the story.

follow in someone's footsteps choose the same career as your father, mother, or other person

reason with try to change someone's opinion

I see. I understand.

world revolves around someone all attention goes to

come to light become known

deal openly speak the truth

7. Literary Term: Irony

Irony is when something happens that is different from what the readers or characters in a story understand or expect to happen. In this story, the author uses family secrets to create some irony.

Focus As you read the story, think about the characters and the secrets they keep from each other. Think about the characters' expectations. What truth do they learn by the end of the story? Do all the characters learn the truth?

About the Author

Henry James (1843–1916) was born in New York City. His parents were wealthy and encouraged their children to get a good education. James started Harvard Law School in 1862. However, he became more interested in writing book reviews and stories and gave up his law studies.

James traveled to Europe several times as a child. As an adult, he briefly tried living and writing in Paris, and later he moved permanently to London. As an American living in Europe, James wrote about the conflict between American and European manners and customs. This theme occurs in many of his novels and short stories. Some of his most famous novels are *The American*, *The Bostonians*, *Washington Square*, and *Daisy Miller*.

The Tree of Knowledge

Audio starts at line 95

Peter Brench was a close friend of Mr. and Mrs. Mallow. The Mallows were married for many years, but Peter was still unmarried at the age
5 of fifty. Peter was in love with Mrs. Mallow, yet he never told her. In fact, he never married because of his love for her. Instead, he spent almost every day with the couple. They ate dinners
10 together and traveled together.

Mr. Mallow was a sculptor. He was able to have a career as an artist because Mrs. Mallow was wealthy. Peter liked Mr. Mallow, but he thought his sculptures were terrible. 15

Peter never told his friends the truth. He never showed his dislike for Mr. Mallow's art or his love for Mrs. Mallow. Thus, Peter was the perfect friend. 20

The Mallows had a son named Lance. They asked Peter to be his godfather. Peter agreed, and he loved his godson.

Lance grew up thinking he would 25 be an artist like his father, and Mrs. Mallow encouraged Lance to follow in his father's footsteps. Lance loved painting, so he wanted to become a painter.

Mrs. Mallow felt Lance had inherited his father's passion, and he might even be a famous artist someday. On the other hand, Peter discouraged painting as a career for his godson. He wanted Lance to study for a career in law or banking at Cambridge University. Peter studied at Cambridge University when he was young. As a result, he asked the university to accept Lance, and the university agreed.

"I was hoping he would lose interest in painting. Being an artist isn't a good career for him."

"But why not, Peter? Why shouldn't he create art?" asked Mrs. Mallow. "Look at the joy his father has in making his sculptures."

"Do you think he'll be like his father?" asked Peter.

"Lance has passion. Some people may criticize his art one day, yet his passion will be stronger than the criticism. He'll find happiness in his work."

Eventually, Peter stopped trying to reason with Mrs. Mallow because Lance had now become a student at Cambridge University.

Soon, however, it was clear that Lance wasn't a very good student. He still thought about painting, and he decided to leave the university and go to Paris to become an artist.

Lance asked Peter, "Do you think I have talent?"

Peter put his arm around Lance and said, "How do I know?"

"Are you saying you can't judge my talent?" Lance continued.

"No, I think that becoming an artist would not be a good life for you. Furthermore, if you decide to give up Paris and stay at Cambridge, I will pay all of your tuition."

"Don't you want me to go to Paris?"

"I think Paris will be wrong for you."

"But why do you want me to stay at home?"

"The four of us are so good together. We are safe together. Let's not spoil it."

"Then what career will I have?"

"I'll take care of you."

"Do you think there's something wrong with me? Do you think I can't become a success?"

"Well, what is a success?"

"I guess people who do what they want to do like my father does. He is happy; therefore, he is successful."

Finally, Lance left Cambridge and went to Paris. He studied art seriously. Occasionally, he came home to visit. A year later, on one of his visits, he had a long talk with Peter about his experience.

"Peter, now I know why you didn't want me to go to Paris to study art. Something terrible has happened to me."

"What is it, my boy? I see from your face that you're not very happy."

The enthusiasm Lance had before going to Paris was gone.

"I'm a terrible artist, Peter. I realize that now. It's a big disappointment to me. I thought the artist's life would be mine. Now, I have nothing. Do you know what I found out in Paris? I learned what I cannot do. In addition, I compared my father's sculptures with other sculptures I saw, and I could see that my father is not a good artist at all. Is that why you didn't want me to go to Paris?"

Peter stared at him. Peter had never discussed Mallow's sculptures with Lance. He thought that Lance, like his mother, believed Mallow was a talented artist. Now Peter understood that Lance knew the truth.

Lance looked at Peter and said, "Do you think I didn't know about my father's lack of talent? Even before I went to Paris and saw great art, I knew my father was not very good. My parents want people to believe my father is a master; however, for a long time, I've known that my father is not good enough to be a master. My father is a dreamer, and my mother feeds his dreams."

■ ■ ■

Peter had never discussed Mallow's sculptures with Lance. He thought that Lance, like his mother, believed Mallow was a talented artist. Now Peter understood that Lance knew the truth.

■ ■ ■

Peter said, "Why didn't you tell me this before?"

Lance answered, "Why did *you* keep your knowledge a secret from *me* for so many years?"

"I did it for your mother."

"Oh, I see."

"Now Lance, you must promise to never say a word to your mother."

"Are you sure my mother doesn't know?"

"If she does, she's too wonderful."

"You think my mother is wonderful? Have you always loved her?"

Peter didn't say anything for a minute. Then, he lowered his head. "I've loved you all. You're my family."

Lance continued, "Poor, Peter. It must be so hard for you. You've had to keep so many secrets. Now, you have my secrets as well – that I know the truth about my father's lack of talent, and that I am a failure as an artist. My father would be angry if he knew the truth about my failure. I will go back to Paris and try painting again. Maybe this time I will be successful."

Six months later, Lance returned home again. This time, his father wanted to see the work Lance created. Mallow did not expect his son to be a master as he was; nevertheless, he expected Lance to have something to show for all the time he spent in Paris.

After Lance showed his work to his father, he went to see Peter. There were tears in Lance's eyes.

"I don't know how you do it, Peter. How do you pretend my father's work is good? I had to show my father all my work. At the same time, I had to pretend that his work is better than mine and that he is a master. Doesn't it make you sad to pretend all the time? I know you love my mother, but she only cares about my father. She loves us, but her world revolves around him."

Peter smiled sadly, "That's how it should be. I don't tell her the truth because I know how much she cares about him. I protect her; therefore, you must protect her as well."

"Dear Peter, I think it's time for you to know. My mother does know the truth. She came to my room yesterday and spent an hour talking to me. She does know about my father. She has always known. All these years she has been pretending, too. She has pretended he was a great artist to protect him.

"All these secrets we kept from each other have finally come to light. Now we are free and perhaps, we can deal openly with each other. Knowledge may be dangerous, but it can also bring us closer. So you see, Peter, your original reason to keep me away from Paris was to keep me from gaining knowledge. You didn't want me to know the truth about my father or about my mother. But I do know."

After that, Lance left the room with a smile on his face and a new joy in his soul. He was now a man, and Peter was proud of him.

Peter remained silent. He thought to himself, "Maybe my original reason to keep Lance away from Paris was to keep myself from gaining knowledge. Maybe I never wanted to know the truth."

1. Understanding the Story

With a partner or in a small group, discuss the following questions.

1. Why does Peter Brench spend so much time with the Mallows?
2. Why does Mrs. Mallow want Lance to become an artist?
3. Why doesn't Peter want Lance to become an artist?
4. What does Lance learn in Paris?
5. What secret has Mrs. Mallow kept for many years?

2. Vocabulary Comprehension

The words on the left are in the story. Match each word to the correct definition on the right. Write the letter of the definition on the blank line.

_f_	1. terrible	a. doing well at something; reaching a goal
_____	2. encourage	b. very good
_____	3. discourage	c. find bad things about someone or something
_____	4. joy	d. money for a college education
_____	5. criticize	e. look for the good or bad in something and give an opinion about it
_____	6. judge	f. very bad
_____	7. tuition	g. give someone hope; tell someone to keep trying to do something
_____	8. success	
_____	9. enthusiasm	h. prevent someone or something from being hurt
_____	10. compare	i. not doing well at something; not reaching a goal
_____	11. truth	j. great interest or energy about something
_____	12. wonderful	k. great happiness
_____	13. failure	l. not give someone hope; tell someone to stop trying to do something
_____	14. protect	m. consider how one thing is similar or equal to another thing
		n. fact

3. Grammar: Connecting Sentences

Writers sometimes connect a simple sentence (a sentence with one independent clause – see page 138) to another simple sentence to make a *complex sentence*. When writers connect two sentences, they show a relationship between them. Two ways to connect sentences are to use *conjunctions* or *transitions*.

- The seven basic conjunctions are *and, but, so, or, nor, for,* and *yet*. Use a comma (,) before the conjunction when it joins two independent clauses.

  Examples:

  Peter was in love with Mrs. Mallow, but he never told her.

  (complete thought with a subject and verb + another complete thought with a subject and verb)

  Lance returned home, and his father wanted to see the work he created.

- Some common transition words are listed below. Use a comma (,) after the transition word. Note that a semicolon (;) or a period (.) must come before the transition word.

  1. To add more information, use words like *in fact, in addition, furthermore, for example, also.*

  2. To show a contrast, use words like *instead, however, nevertheless, on the other hand.*

  3. To show a result, use words like *therefore, as a result, thus.*

  4. To show time, use words like *eventually, occasionally, first, second, then, later, now, finally, at the same time.*

  Examples:

  Mrs. Mallow encouraged Lance to be an artist. However, Peter discouraged this career for his godson.
  (*However* shows a contrast between Mrs. Mallow's idea and Peter's idea.)

  Peter liked Mr. Mallow; therefore, he couldn't tell him that he didn't like his sculptures.
  (*Therefore* shows the result of Peter's friendship – he can't tell his friend the truth.)

■ *Practice 1*

The following sentences and clauses are from the story. Without looking back at the story, choose the correct words to connect them.

1. Peter was in love with Mrs. Mallow, _____ (*and* / *yet* / *so*) he never told her. _____ (*Nevertheless,* / *Finally,* / *In fact,*) he never married because of his love for her.

2. Mr. Mallow was a sculptor. . . . Peter liked Mr. Mallow, _____ (*so* / *and* / *but*) he thought his sculptures were terrible.

3. "Lance has passion. Some people may criticize his art one day, _____ (*so* / *yet* / *or*) his passion will be stronger than the criticism."

4. Finally, Lance left Cambridge and went to Paris. . . . _____ (*In addition,* / *Occasionally,* / *As a result,*) he came home to visit.

5. "In addition, I compared my father's sculptures with other sculptures I saw, _____ (*but* / *so* / *and*) I could see that my father is not a good artist at all."

■ *Practice 2*

Connect the following sentences. Use conjunctions or transitions. Use the comma, semicolon, or period correctly.

1. Peter is 50 years old. He has never been married.

   _____

2. Peter spends a lot of time with the Mallows. He is not a member of the family.

   _____

3. Peter loves Lance. He wants to protect him from the truth.

   _____

4. Lance finds the truth in Paris. His mother tells him her secret about his father.

   _____

5. Lance becomes a man. Peter is very proud of him.

   _____

D | THINKING ABOUT THE STORY

1. Sharing Ideas

With a partner or in a small group, discuss the following questions.

1. What are Peter's secrets about the Mallows? Why doesn't he tell anyone his secrets?
2. Do you think Mr. and Mrs. Mallow have a good relationship? Why or why not?
3. How does Lance change after he goes to Paris?
4. What do you think Lance means when he tells Peter that knowledge can be dangerous, but it can also bring people closer together?
5. Which character in the story do you like best? Why do you like that character?

2. Reading Between the Lines

Authors often write something that can have more than one meaning. You need to figure out what the author means. This is called *reading between the lines*. Read the following sentences from the story. Then circle the answer that shows the author's meaning. If you need help, look back at the story. Discuss your answers.

1. "Do you think he'll be like his father?" asked Peter.

   a. Peter thinks that Lance will become a sculptor.

   b. Peter thinks that Lance should be a banker.

   c. Peter is worried that Lance will have no talent because his father has no talent.

2. "The four of us are so good together. We are safe together. Let's not spoil it."

   a. Peter does not want Lance to go to Paris because Paris is dangerous.

   b. Peter does not want Lance to go to Paris because Lance and the Mallows are like a close family.

   c. Peter will be angry with Lance if Lance goes to Paris.

3. "My father is a dreamer, and my mother feeds his dreams."

   a. Lance feels that his mother will do anything to encourage her husband.

   b. Lance thinks that his mother gives his father lots of money.

   c. Lance thinks that his mother cooks delicious meals for her husband.

3. Analyzing the Story: Irony

As you read on page 144, *irony* can be how readers or characters see or understand the truth. On the left side of the chart are secrets or beliefs. On the right side of the chart are the ironies of the secrets or beliefs. Fill in the blank lines to complete each sentence.

THE SECRETS AND BELIEFS	THE IRONY
Peter Brench loves Mrs. Mallow and thinks it is a secret.	However, ____*everyone knows*____ that Peter loves her.
Peter Brench doesn't want Lance to know that his father is a terrible artist.	Nevertheless, Lance _____ that his father is not a good artist.
Mr. Mallow thinks that he, himself, is a good artist.	On the other hand, everyone else thinks _____.
Peter Brench thinks he is protecting Mrs. Mallow by not telling her that her husband's art is terrible.	However, Mrs. Mallow doesn't need Peter's protection because she _____ _____.

4. Summary

Put the following sentences in the correct order to summarize the story. Write the numbers 1 to 6 to show the order. The first one has been done for you.

_____ Lance realizes he's not a good artist.

_____ Lance gains knowledge about himself and his family's secrets.

___1___ Peter Brench is a close friend of the Mallow family.

_____ Lance wants to be an artist like his father.

_____ Peter becomes the godfather to the Mallows' son Lance.

_____ Peter doesn't want Lance to study art in Paris.

5. Writing

Continue the story. Pretend it is five years later. What has happened to Mr. and Mrs. Mallow, Lance, and Peter? Describe their relationships with each other.

Chapter 12

All the Years of Her Life MORLEY CALLAGHAN

A PRE-READING

1. Think Before you Read

Answer the following questions.

1. Why do you think some people steal – take things from other people or places without paying for them?
2. What should employers do if one of their employees steals things from them?
3. What should parents do when their children steal?

2. Picture Focus

With a partner, talk about the picture.

Who are the three people? What are the man and woman talking about?

3. Key Vocabulary

Study the following key words and expressions from the story. They all relate to *stealing*. Then complete the paragraph using each word or expression once.

> **nervous** worried or frightened
>
> **thief** a person who steals something
>
> **robs** steals something from someone or some place
>
> **arrest** when the police take a person and put him or her in jail
>
> **jail** a place that the police use for people who have been arrested
>
> **caught red-handed** when someone is found doing something wrong

There are many different types of stealing. Some people take small things from family or friends. Other people steal from their employers or shoplift from stores. A _____ is a person who usually makes a career out of stealing. He or she often _____ houses or banks and does not get _____ easily. This type of person keeps stealing until he or she is _____ _____. If this happens, and the police come to the scene, the police will _____ this person and put him or her in _____.

4. Story Preview 🎧

Read the preview of the story. Then answer the questions in *Making Predictions* on the next page.

> Alfred, a teenage boy who has left school, gets into trouble when he is caught stealing from his employer, Mr. Carr. His mother comes to help him as she has done many times before. But this time, Alfred is surprised by how calm she is. When they walk home, Alfred's mother is quiet and doesn't speak to him. She acts as if he isn't walking next to her.

5. Making Predictions

From the *Story Preview*, try to predict what will happen. Circle one choice below or write your own answer. Discuss your predictions with a partner.

What will Alfred's mother do when they get home?

1. She will tell Alfred to leave home.

2. She will never speak to Alfred again.

3. She will tell Alfred's father about the stealing.

4. _____

6. Idioms and Expressions

You will find these idioms and expressions in the story.

---

just a moment a short time; people say this or "just a minute" when they want someone to wait

catch your breath return to normal breathing after excitement or activity

get in trouble do something wrong

hold a job have a job; keep working at a job

hang around with spend a lot of time with someone

fire someone when an employer tells someone to leave a job because the person did something bad

Thank goodness! people say this when they are happy that something good happened that they expected to be bad

---

7. Literary Term: Tone

Tone shows the writer's feelings about the subject and characters of the story. The tone may be happy or sad, calm or angry, funny or serious. Through description and dialogue, the writer sets, or creates, the tone.

Focus   As you read the story, think about the tone of the story. Is there more than one tone? Notice the descriptions and dialogues that help set the tone of the story. Notice if the tone changes during the story.

About the Author

Morley Edward Callaghan (1903–1990) was born and raised in Toronto, Ontario. He attended the University of Toronto Law School, but he never practiced law. Instead, he became a newspaper reporter for the Toronto *Daily Star*. Callaghan became friends with the famous American author Ernest Hemingway, who was working in Canada at the time as a reporter. It was Hemingway who encouraged Callaghan to write short stories.

After Callaghan married, he and his wife went to Paris. They spent several months in Paris and were part of a group of writers that included Hemingway, James Joyce, and F. Scott Fitzgerald. During this time in Paris, Hemingway challenged Callaghan to a fighting match. Callaghan, who had been a fighter in college, knocked Hemingway to the ground, and Hemingway never forgave him.

Callaghan wrote short stories, short novels, and nonfiction. He became a well-known writer in Canada and the United States. One of his two sons, Barry Callaghan, also became a writer and poet. He wrote about his father in *Barrelhouse Kings* (1998).

All the Years of Her Life

Audio starts at line 161

Alfred Higgins worked in a drugstore. One night, as he was getting ready to leave for the day, he took off his white jacket and put on his coat. Sam Carr, who owned the drugstore, was standing near the cash register.[1] Most nights, he didn't look at Alfred and just said, "Good night." Tonight, he said softly, "Just a moment, Alfred. Just a moment before you go."

Alfred started to button his coat and felt nervous. His heart began

[1] *cash register*: a machine used in stores for keeping money from a sale or giving money as change

to beat so loud it was hard for him to catch his breath. "What is it, Mr. Carr?"

"Maybe you should take a few things out of your pocket before you go," said Mr. Carr.

"What things? What are you talking about?"

"You have a compact[2] and a lipstick and two tubes of toothpaste in your pocket, Alfred."

"What do you mean? Are you calling me a thief?" Alfred's face got red, and he knew he looked insulted. Sam Carr's blue eyes were shining behind his glasses, and his lips were moving underneath his gray mustache. He nodded his head a few times, and Alfred became frightened. Slowly he put his hand in the deep pocket of his coat. He never looked at Sam Carr's eyes as he took out a compact, a lipstick, and two tubes of toothpaste. He put them one by one on the counter.

"How long have you been stealing from me?" asked Mr. Carr.

"This is the first time I took anything, Mr. Carr."

"Do you expect me to believe that? You've probably been robbing the store for a while. I liked you, Alfred. I trusted you, and now, I'll have to call a policeman. You're a fool, and maybe I should call your father and tell him you're a fool. Maybe I should let him know I'm going to have you arrested and put in jail."

"My father's not at home. He's a printer, and he works nights," said Alfred.

"Who's at home?"

"My mother, I guess."

"Then we'll see what she says," and he went to the telephone and dialed her number.

■ ■ ■

"How long have you been stealing from me?"

■ ■ ■

"Just a minute. Do you have to tell her?"

He wanted to sound like a big guy who could take care of himself, but there was still a childish hope that someone at home would come and help him.

Alfred left school and lived at home with his parents. His older brothers were married and his sister just got married, so it was finally easier for his parents. But Alfred always got in trouble and couldn't hold a job for very long.

"Yes, that's right, Mrs. Higgins. Your boy's in trouble, I'm afraid. You better come here in a hurry." Alfred heard Mr. Carr speaking to his mother.

Alfred knew his mother would come rushing in. Maybe she would be crying, and she would push him away when he tried to talk to her. Yet he hoped she would arrive before Mr.

2 *compact*: a small box for women's face powder

Carr saw the policeman who usually walked by the store.

While they waited, they didn't speak. Then they heard someone tapping on the glass door. Mr. Carr opened the door and said, "Come in, Mrs. Higgins." He looked angry.

Mrs. Higgins looked as if she was going to bed when she got the phone call. Her hair was tied and covered with a hat. Her coat was wrapped around her tightly. She was large and round and had a friendly smile on her face. Most of the store lights were turned off, and at first, she didn't see Alfred. He was standing in the dark at the end of the counter. When she saw him, she looked at him with her blue eyes and smiled. She was calm and dignified. She gave Mr. Carr her hand and said, "I'm Mrs. Higgins. I'm Alfred's mother. Is he in trouble?"

Mr. Carr was a little surprised by her lack of fear. "He is. He's been stealing from the store. I caught him red-handed. He took little things like compacts, toothpaste, and lipstick. It's stuff he can sell easily."

"Is it true, Alfred?"

"Yes."

"Why have you been doing it?"

"I wanted to have more money, I guess."

"For what?"

"When I hang around with the guys, I guess."

Mrs. Higgins touched Mr. Carr's arm gently and spoke as though she didn't want to disturb him. She was serious and shy as she asked, "What did you plan to do, Mr. Carr?"

"I was going to call a policeman. That's what I should do."

"Yes, maybe. I can't tell you what to do because he's my son. Yet sometimes I think a little good advice is the best thing for a boy when he's at a certain period of his life."

Alfred was amazed at his mother's quiet behavior. If they were at home and someone said Alfred was going to be arrested, she would be crying. Yet here she was standing there with a gentle smile on her face saying, "Maybe it would be better to just let him come home with me. He looks like a big fellow, doesn't he? It takes some of them a long time to get any sense."

Both adults looked at Alfred. Alfred felt uncomfortable. He knew Mr. Carr realized that his mother was really a fine woman. There was only the sound of his mother's soft, confident voice in the store. Without being excited or frightened, Mrs. Higgins showed dignity in the dark store.

Mr. Carr nodded his head. "Of course, I want to help him learn to do what is right. I tell you what I'll do. I'll just fire him and I won't tell the police. Okay?" Then he shook hands with Mrs. Higgins.

"I'll never forget your kindness, Mr. Carr," she said.

"Sorry we had to meet this way."

They acted as if they liked each other, as if they had known each other a long time. "Good night, sir."

"Good night, Mrs. Higgins. I'm truly sorry."

The mother and son walked along the street together. Mrs. Higgins took long steps, and her serious face looked worried. Alfred was afraid to speak to her. He was afraid of the silence between them. The longer they walked in silence, the more he realized how strong his mother was. He wondered what she was thinking. She seemed to forget that he was walking beside her. Finally, he said, "Thank goodness it turned out like that. I certainly won't get in trouble like that again."

"Be quiet. Don't speak to me. You've disgraced me again and again," she said angrily.

"That's the last time. That's all I'm saying, Mom."

When they arrived home and his mother took off her coat, Alfred saw that she had put on a dress quickly before she went to the store. "You're a bad one. You are always in trouble. Why do you stand there? Go to bed. I'm going to make a cup of tea. Remember now, don't say anything about tonight to your father."

Alfred went upstairs and got undressed. He heard his mother in the kitchen filling the tea kettle, putting it on the stove, and moving a chair. He could remember Mr. Carr listening to her talk simply. Alfred felt a pride in her strength and calmness when she spoke to Mr. Carr. "I'd like to tell her she was great with Mr. Carr."

Alfred went downstairs to the kitchen. He watched his mother pour a cup of tea. He watched silently as his mother sat there. Her face was frightened and not like the face of the woman who was so confident before in the drugstore.

When she reached for the kettle, her hand was trembling and she spilled some water on the stove. Leaning back in the chair, she sighed and lifted the cup to her lips. She swallowed the hot tea. Then she sat up straight, though her hand still trembled. She looked very old.

Alfred realized that his mother always trembled whenever he was in trouble. This trembling had been inside her when she rushed to the drugstore. He watched his mother, and he didn't speak, but at that moment, his youth seemed to be over. All the years of her life showed in her trembling hand as she raised the cup to her lips. This seemed to be the first time he ever really looked at his mother.

1. Understanding the Story

With a partner or in a small group, discuss the following questions.

1. How does Alfred act when Mr. Carr asks him to take things out of his pocket?
2. How does Alfred expect his mother to act when she comes to the drugstore?
3. What does Mrs. Higgins say to Mr. Carr? Is Alfred surprised?
4. How does Mrs. Higgins behave when she and Alfred walk home?
5. What does Alfred notice about his mother when she is drinking her tea?

2. Vocabulary Comprehension

The words in the list and the sentences that follow are in the story. Read the sentences and circle the letter of the best meaning of the **bold** word in each sentence.

insulted	calm	stuff	confident	trembling
tapping	dignified	disturb	kindness	sighed
wrapped	surprised	sense	disgraced	swallowed

1. Alfred's face got red, and he knew he looked **insulted**.
   a. like he had a fever   c. afraid of Mr. Carr
   b. unhappy with what Mr. Carr said

2. Then they heard someone **tapping** on the glass door.
   a. dancing   c. knocking
   b. writing

3. Her coat was **wrapped** around her tightly.
   a. papered   c. open
   b. covered

4. She was **calm** and dignified.
   a. excited   c. relaxed
   b. nervous

5. She was calm and **dignified**.
   a. respectable   c. charming
   b. lonely

6. Mr. Carr was a little **surprised** by her lack of fear.
   a. amazed
   b. happy
   c. excited

7. "It's **stuff** he can sell easily."
   a. food
   b. things
   c. old items

8. Mrs. Higgins touched Mr. Carr's arm gently and spoke as though she didn't want to **disturb** him.
   a. annoy
   b. see
   c. insult

9. "It takes some of them a long time to get any **sense**."
   a. money
   b. good judgment
   c. touch

10. There was only the sound of his mother's soft, **confident** voice in the store.
   a. positive and clear
   b. quiet and scared
   c. clever and encouraging

11. "I'll never forget your **kindness**, Mr. Carr," she said.
   a. family
   b. bravery
   c. goodness

12. "You've **disgraced** me again and again," she said angrily.
   a. made other people hate
   b. made other people lose respect for
   c. made other people uncomfortable with

13. When she reached for the kettle, her hand was **trembling**, and she spilled some water on the stove.
   a. shaking
   b. very hot
   c. not moving

14. Leaning back in the chair, she **sighed** and lifted the cup to her lips.
   a. spoke as she breathed out
   b. made a soft noise as she breathed out
   c. smiled as she breathed out

15. She **swallowed** the hot tea.
   a. spilled
   b. boiled
   c. drank

3. Grammar: Forming Questions

Two types of questions in English are *Yes / No* questions and *Wh-* questions.

■ ***Yes / No* questions can be answered with *yes* or *no*.**

To turn a simple present or simple past statement into a *Yes / No* question, use *do, does,* or *did* + the subject + the main form of the verb.

Examples:
Statement: *Alfred has two tubes of toothpaste in his pocket.*
Question: *<u>Does</u> Alfred <u>have</u> two tubes of toothpaste in his pocket?*
Statement: *Alfred stole the toothpaste from Mr. Carr.*
Question: *<u>Did</u> Alfred <u>steal</u> the toothpaste from Mr. Carr?*

To turn a present continuous or past continuous statement into a *Yes / No* question, change the order of the subject and the *be* verb.

Examples:
Statement: *<u>Mrs. Higgins</u> <u>is</u> talking to Mr. Carr.*
Question: *<u>Is</u> <u>Mrs. Higgins</u> talking to Mr. Carr?*
Statement: *<u>Alfred and his mother</u> <u>were</u> walking silently.*
Question: *<u>Were</u> <u>Alfred and his mother</u> walking silently?*

■ ***Wh-* questions ask for information. They begin with words like *who, what, when, where, why,* and *how.***

To turn a simple present or simple past statement into a *Wh-* question, add a *Wh-* question word + *do, does,* or *did* + the subject + the main form of the verb.

Examples:
Statement: *Alfred has two tubes of toothpaste in his pocket.*
Question: *<u>Why</u> <u>does</u> Alfred <u>have</u> two tubes of toothpaste in his pocket?*
Statement: *Alfred stole the toothpaste from Mr. Carr.*
Question: *<u>What</u> <u>did</u> Alfred <u>steal</u> from Mr. Carr?*

To turn a present continuous or past continuous statement into a *Wh-* question, add a *Wh-* question word and change the order of the subject and the *be* verb.

Example:
Statement: *<u>Mrs. Higgins</u> <u>is</u> talking to Mr. Carr.*
Question: *<u>Why</u> <u>is</u> <u>Mrs. Higgins</u> talking to Mr. Carr?*

■ *Practice 1*

Correct the following questions from the story. Some questions are missing words. Some use the wrong verb form. Some use the wrong word order. Then capitalize the first letter of the question, and put a question mark at the end.

1. what you talking about

   What are you talking about? _____

2. are calling me a thief

   _____

3. you expect me to believe that

   _____

4. do you has to tell her

   _____

5. he is in trouble

   _____

6. what you does plan to do, Mr. Carr

   _____

■ *Practice 2*

Now write two questions to ask Alfred, Mr. Carr, or Mrs. Higgins something about their feelings or actions. Use *Yes / No* or *Wh-* questions.

1. Alfred, _____?

2. Alfred, _____?

3. Mr. Carr, _____?

4. Mr. Carr, _____?

5. Mrs. Higgins, _____?

6. Mrs. Higgins, _____?

1. Sharing Ideas

With a partner or in a small group, discuss the following questions.

1. Why do you think Alfred doesn't want Mr. Carr to call his mother?
2. Do you think Alfred will steal again? Why or why not?
3. Do you think Mr. Carr should have fired Alfred, called the police, or told his father? Explain your answer.
4. What does Alfred understand about his mother and her life when he sees her hand trembling?

2. Reading Between the Lines

Authors often write something that can have more than one meaning. You need to figure out what the author means. This is called *reading between the lines*. Read the following quotes from the story. Then circle the answer that shows the author's meaning. If you need help, look back at the story. Discuss your answers.

1. Alfred says to Mr. Carr, "What do you mean? Are you calling me a thief?"

    a. Alfred pretends he doesn't understand what Mr. Carr is thinking.

    b. Alfred is insulted that Mr. Carr thinks he is a thief.

    c. Alfred hopes Mr. Carr will think he's scared.

2. Alfred asks Mr. Carr, "Do you have to tell her?"

    a. Alfred wants Mr. Carr to call the police instead of his mother.

    b. Alfred knows his mother isn't at home.

    c. Alfred is scared and hopes Mr. Carr will change his mind.

3. On the walk home, Alfred tells his mother, "That's the last time."

    a. Alfred is telling his mother that he will not steal again.

    b. Alfred is lying to his mother.

    c. Alfred doesn't want to talk to his mother anymore.

4. Alfred says, "I'd like to tell her she was great with Mr. Carr."

    a. Alfred's wants his mother to feel proud of him.

    b. Alfred respects the way his mother behaved with Mr. Carr.

    c. Alfred likes Mr. Carr.

3. Analyzing the Story: Tone

As you read on page 156, *tone* shows the writer's feelings about the subject and characters. The writer sets the tone through description and dialogue. Three types of tone from the story are in the chart. Examples of descriptions or dialogue are shown for each type of tone. Read the story again and look for more examples to add to the chart.

TONE of "All the Years of Her Life"		
NERVOUSNESS	**SILENCE**	**ANGER**
"What things? What are you talking about?"	*Mrs. Higgins took long steps, and her serious face looked worried.*	*"Be quiet. Don't speak to me. You've disgraced me again and again."*

4. Summary

Put the following sentences in the correct order to summarize the story. Write the numbers 1 to 6 to show the order. The first one has been done for you.

_____ Mr. Carr calls Mrs. Higgins on the telephone.

_____ Alfred and his mother walk home in silence.

___1___ Mr. Carr accuses Alfred of stealing from the store.

_____ Mrs. Higgins is calm and dignified in the store.

_____ Mr. Carr agrees not to call the police.

_____ Alfred watches his mother drink the tea with a trembling hand.

5. Writing

Pretend you are Alfred. Write a letter to Mr. Carr. Explain how sorry you are about stealing from him and about the lesson you learned.

Summing Up

A | TAKE A CLOSER LOOK

1. Theme Comparison: Close Relationships

The three stories in Part Four describe the happiness, disappointment, secrets, and conflicts the characters have with each other. They also describe the knowledge the characters gain about themselves and about each other. Pan discovers who she is and learns the meaning of betrayal. Peter Brench understands that he does not want to accept the truth of his secrets. Alfred realizes the pain he has caused his mother.

With a partner, discuss the following questions.

1. How does Mark destroy his close relationship with Pan?
2. In what ways does Peter prove to be a good friend to the Mallows?
3. How do you think Mrs. Higgins feels about her son and about her life?

2. Freewriting

Write the words *close relationships* at the top of a sheet of paper. Then write any words that come into your mind when you think of *close relationships*. For 15 minutes, write about the close relationships in your life. Who are the people closest to you? How do they make you feel? What have you learned from them? Have they ever disappointed you? Have you ever disappointed them?

B | REVIEW

1. Grammar Review

Connect the following pairs of sentences to create a one-paragraph summary of the three stories in Part Four. Use the conjunctions and transitions in Chapter 11.

The characters in Part Four had conflicts. There was also love in their relationships.

Pan was betrayed by Mark. He expected Pan to love him.

Mrs. Mallow loved her husband. She pretended his art was good.

Alfred was proud of his mother. He was amazed at her dignity.

2. Vocabulary Review

The definitions under *Across* and *Down* are for vocabulary words in Part Four. Read the definitions and complete the crossword puzzle with the correct vocabulary words.

Across
2. practices or habits of a person, group, or country
5. find bad things about someone or something
7. say or think that someone is responsible for something bad that happened
8. prevent someone or thing from being hurt
10. give someone hope; tell someone to keep trying
12. well-known by many people
14. annoy

Down
1. concerned about a problem or something about to happen
3. sign that is used to represent something else
4. shaky; thinking about something about to happen, like a test
5. find the similarities or sameness between two things
6. quick intelligence or problem solving
9. relaxed
11. when the police take a person and put him or her in jail
13. good judgment

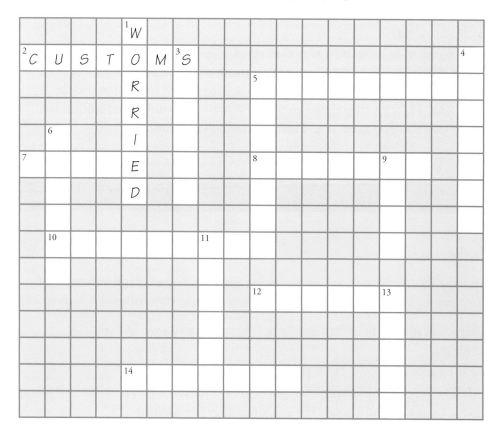

Filling Out the Elements Chart

This chart shows the five basic elements of a short story. You can find definitions for these elements on page 170. Some of these elements have been filled out for "Its Wavering Image." Complete the chart. Then copy the blank chart on page xvii and fill it out for "The Tree of Knowledge" or "All the Years of Her Life" or for both stories. Share your charts with a partner or in a small group.

Elements of _____ Its Wavering Image _____
(name of story)

SETTING
Chinatown in Montreal, Canada

CHARACTERS
Pan, Man Yu, Mark Carson

PLOT

CONFLICT

THEME(S)

Appendix

Atmosphere The feelings or mood of a story are called the atmosphere.

Characters The people in a story are called the characters. The most important people in a story are the main characters. Other people in the story are minor characters.

Conflict Within a plot there is often a conflict, or struggle. The conflict can be between characters, between a character and the environment, or within a character's mind.

Foreshadowing The hints and clues that an author puts in a story to prepare you for what is going to happen in the story are called foreshadowing.

Irony In literature, irony is when there is a difference between what is expected and what actually happens.

Local Color Anything in a story that helps give readers a clear picture of what the life and times of the story were like is called the local color.

Plot The plot is the events that happen from the beginning of a story to the end.

Sensory Details An author gives you sensory details to create images of the five senses – *touch, taste, smell, sight,* and *sound.* These help describe a story.

Setting The setting is the time and the place of a story.

Surprise Ending A surprise ending is a sudden or unexpected ending.

Theme A story's theme is the main idea of the plot. Sometimes a story has several themes.

Tone The tone shows the writer's feelings about the subject and characters of a story. The tone may be happy or sad, calm or angry, funny or serious.

VOCABULARY

The following list is the vocabulary from the activities in this book. The items are listed in their dictionary forms. Chapter numbers are next to each item.

WORDS

addition 3
adopt 4
adventure 1
allow 4
amazed 2
angry 6
anniversary 7
approach 5
arrest 12
assignment 1
attract 10
awaken 5
balance 3
bargain 2
behavior 6
belief 10
belong 10
bet 4
betray 10
blame 10
blood 8
blush 2
boast 9
borrow 9
bow 2
bravest 4
bury 9
calm 12
carriage 5
castle 8
celebrate 7
change 2
character 5
charming 5
clever 10
comfort 10
communicate 6
compare 11
confident 12

content 1
contribution 4
cottage 7
couple 6
courage 6
coward 6
cozy 7
create 11
creek 4
criminal 4
criticize 11
custom 10
deceased 3
decorate 7
degree 1
detail 3
dignified 12
disappearance 7
disappointed 7
discourage 11
disgrace 12
distance 6
disturb 12
dizzy 8
dream 1
drift 4
drunk 5
editor 10
encourage 11
energy 6
entertain 8
enthusiasm 11
ethnicity 10
evil 5
expect 7
failure 11
famous 11
flame 8
floral 7

foolish 5
foreign 10
fortunate 4
fortune 3
frightened 8
funeral 4
gamble 4
gate 8
generous 2
ghost 9
grab 8
grade 1
grave 8
habit 1
handsome 5
hang 8
haunt 9
heir 3
hope 4
horrify 8
horror 8
human 7
improve 4
inherit 3
innocent 5
insult 12
interrupt 3
invest 3
invite 7
jail 12
jealous 9
joke 3
journalist 10
joy 11
judge 11
kindness 12
knowledge 1
lawyer 3
lean 2

leave 3
literature 1
log cabin 7
lonely 1
loose 9
lucky charm 4
luxury 2
manners 9
marvelous 8
master 11
miracle 1
mysterious 9
narrow 6
nervous 12
nod 5
nonsense 6
obey 6
pace 6
painter 11
passenger 5
passion 6
pillow 5
pleasant 2
politely 3
practical 2
pretend 6
pride 2
promise 10
protect 11
pumpkin 9
realize 1
reduce 2
reflection 10
remind 3
rob 12
rule 8
rush 8
saddle 9
sale 2

save 2
scarf 7
scholar 1
sculptor 11
sculpture 11
search 9
secret 1
sense 12
seriously 3
sheet 8
shy 4
sigh 12
sleepy 5
smile 6
soldier 9

soul 1
spoil 1
stare 1, 2
steal 1
strange 1
stuff 12
success 11
suffer 8
superstitious 9
surprised 12
swallow 12
sweep 4
symbol 10
tale 9
talent 11

tap 12
taste 7
tear 7
tent 7
terrible 11
thief 12
thunder 9
towel 7
treasure 2
tremble 12
trusted 10
truth 11
tuition 11
unaware 5
unselfishly 3

valley 9
victim 8
wallet 2
warning 6
washstand 7
waver 10
welcome 10
whistle 3
will 3
wish 2
wonder 4
wonderful 11
worried 10
wrap 12
yawn 1

Idioms and Expressions

at home with 10
be worth 3
better days 2
board a train 1
break up 9
bring good luck 4
business as usual 6
catch red-handed 12
catch up (with s/o) 6
catch your breath 12
check your watch 7
(the) clock strikes 8
come to light 11
come to the rescue 6
deal openly 11
depend on 3
don't fit in 1
Don't you dare! 10
drop by 7
facial feature 10
fall asleep 5
fall in love 6
feast on 9
feel sorry for someone 7
fire someone 12
follow in someone's
    footsteps 11
gain courage 8
get in trouble 12
get there in plenty of
    time 1

get tired of 1
give birth 4
go on stage 3
goose bumps 9
(a) great deal of 4
hang around with 12
have in mind 5
have no right 10
hold a job 12
hold hands 6
How dare you! 8
I see. 11
I'll bet you. 5
I'll take this. 2
just a moment 12
keep someone company 7
like a thief in the night 8
lose its magic 1
make a living 5
make eyes at 6
make fun of 8
marriage proposal 9
May I help you? 2
mouth watering 9
on foot 5
on sale 2
one by one 4
out of sight 5
pass an exam 1
pay attention to 3
play tricks on (someone) 9

pull through 4
reason with 11
run away together 6
sell one's soul 10
send regards 7
(a) shady spot 5
sharp pain 8
show no sign of 4
show off 6
shy away from 10
sleep soundly 5
sun goes down 1
take a close look at 4
take a nap 5
take a seat 2
take off (leave quickly –
    depart) 6
take turns 7
Thank goodness! 12
turn white 3
wake up 5
walk arm in arm 1
watch every penny 2
wild and scary 8
(a) woman's touch 7
world revolves around
    someone 11
would rather 10
Would you mind? 3

Credits

The 12 short stories in *Discovering Fiction, An Introduction*, have been adapted from the originals. You can find the originals in the following publications.

Sinclair Lewis, "Young Man Axelbrod," from *Selected Short Stories of Sinclair Lewis*. Published by Doubleday, Doran, Garden City, New York, 1935.

Kate Chopin, "A Pair of Silk Stockings," from *Bayou Folk*. Published by Houghton Mifflin & Co, Boston and New York, 1894.

O. Henry, "One Thousand Dollars," from *Introducing the Short Story*, edited by Christ and Shostak. Published by Amsco School Publications, Inc., New York, 1991.

Bret Harte, "The Luck of Roaring Camp," from *The Luck of Roaring Camp and Other Tales*. Published by Dodd, Mead, New York, 1961.

Nathaniel Hawthorne, "David Swan," from *Twice Told Tales*. Published by Maynard, Merrill & Co., New York, 1897. First published in *The Token and Atlantic Souvenir*, Boston, 1837.

Stephen Crane, "The Pace of Youth," from *Great Short Works of Stephen Crane*. Published by Perennial Press (a Harper Collins publication), New York, 2004. First published in the *New York Press*, New York, January 1895.

Mark Twain, "The Californian's Tale." First published in *Harper's Magazine*, New York, 1902.

Edgar Allan Poe, "The Mask of the Red Death," from *The Mask of the Red Death: An Edgar Allan Poe Mystery* by Harold Schector. Published by Ballantine Books, New York, 2004.

Washington Irving, "The Legend of Sleepy Hollow," from *The Complete Tales of Washington Irving*. Published by Doubleday & Co., Garden City, New York, 1975.

Edith Eaton, "Its Wavering Image," from *Mrs. Spring Fragrance and Other Writings*, edited by Amy Ling and Annette White-Parks. Published by Urbana, University of Illinois, 1995.

Henry James, "The Tree of Knowledge," from *The Best Short Stories of the Modern Age* by Douglas Angus. Published by Ballantine, New York, 1987.

Morley Callaghan, "All the Years of Her Life," from *Now That April's Here and Other Stories*. Published by Random House, New York, 1936. Reprinted with permission from Barry Callaghan, 2007.

Index

Track List for Audio CD

The audio CD includes the Story Previews and excerpts from all the stories in *Discovering Fiction, An Introduction.*

TRACK	CHAPTER	SELECTION	PAGES
1		Introduction	
2	1	Story Preview	5
3	1	*Young Man Axelbrod* – lines 113–242	9–10
4	2	Story Preview	17
5	2	*A Pair of Silk Stockings* – lines 37–131	20–21
6	3	Story Preview	29
7	3	*One Thousand Dollars* – lines 22–164	31–33
8	4	Story Preview	47
9	4	*The Luck of Roaring Camp* – lines 44–132	50–51
10	5	Story Preview	59
11	5	*David Swan* – lines 26–112	62–63
12	6	Story Preview	71
13	6	*The Pace of Youth* – lines 54–170	74–75
14	7	Story Preview	89
15	7	*The Californian's Tale* – lines 76–174	92–93
16	8	Story Preview	101
17	8	*The Mask of the Red Death* – lines 26–121	103–105
18	9	Story Preview	113
19	9	*The Legend of Sleepy Hollow* – lines 124–189	117–118
20	10	Story Preview	131
21	10	*Its Wavering Image* – lines 42–154	134–135
22	11	Story Preview	143
23	11	*The Tree of Knowledge* – lines 95–219	147–148
24	12	Story Preview	155
25	12	*All the Years of Her Life* – lines 161–223	160